Contents

HOW TO BE HAPPY THOUGH MARRIED

Handbook to Marriage

"Domestic happiness, thou only bliss
Of Paradise that hast survived the fall!
Though few now taste thee, unimpaired and pure,
Or, tasting, long enjoy thee, too infirm
Or too incautious to preserve thy sweets
Unmixed with drops of bitters, which neglect
Or temper sheds into thy crystal cup."—*Cowper.*

"It is fit that I should infuse a bunch of myrrh into the festival goblet, and, after the Egyptian manner, serve up a dead man's bones at a feast: I will only show it, and take it away again; it will make the wine bitter, but wholesome."—*Jeremy Taylor.*

TO THOSE BRAVE MEN AND WOMEN WHO HAVE VENTURED, OR WHO INTEND TO VENTURE, INTO THAT STATE WHICH IS "A BLESSING TO A FEW, A CURSE TO MANY, AND A GREAT UNCERTAINTY TO ALL," THIS BOOK IS RESPECTFULLY DEDICATED IN ADMIRATION OF THEIR COURAGE.

PREFACE.

Most of the books intended to give "counsel and ghostly strength" to newly-married people are so like a collection of sermons that they are given away rather than read. When writing the following pages I have remembered that the only kind of vice all people agree to shun is—advice, and have endeavoured to hide the pill. This is my excuse if at times I seem to fall into anecdotage.

One day two birds were busy building their nest in Luther's garden. Observing that they were often scared while committing their petty thefts by the passers to and fro, the Doctor exclaimed, "Oh, poor little birds! fly not away; I wish you well with all my heart, if you would only believe me!" If any birds of Paradise, or, to speak plainly, newly-married people, are a little scared by the title of this book or by any of its contents, I assure them that, while trying to place before them the responsibilities they have undertaken, I wish them well with all my heart, and take great interest in their nest-building.

To ask critics to be merciful at a time when new books are so numerous that our eyes ache with reading and our fingers with turning the pages, would be to ask them not to do their duty. They are the policemen of literature, and they are bound to make bad and worthless books "move on" out of the way of their betters. I can only hope that if any notice this little venture they may not feel obliged to "crush" it "among the stoure," as the Ayrshire ploughman had to crush the "wee, modest, crimson-tipped flower."

I take this opportunity of thanking M. H., my best friend, without whose help and sympathy this book would be a worse one than it is, and my life much more unsatisfactory.

Part of the first chapter was published in *Chambers's Journal*, and I am indebted to *Cassell's Saturday Journal* for two anecdotes. I now tender my best thanks to the proprietors of those periodicals for permission to reprint the passages.

PREFACE

TO THE SECOND EDITION.

The "wee, modest, crimson-tipped flower," as I called this book when it first made its appearance, has not been crushed with the ploughshare of criticism "among the stoure." On the contrary, it has been so well received that I am full of gratitude to the reviewers who recommended it and to the public who bought it. One critic suggested that to make the work complete a chapter on second marriages should be added. My reason for not writing such a chapter is that, not having myself been as yet often married, I did not presume to give advice to widows and widowers who have their own experience to guide them.

Taking up the book in a lending library a friend read aloud the title to a lady who accompanied her—"How to be Happy though Married." *Lady*: "Oh, bother the happiness; does it tell how to be married?" I hope that I may be pardoned if I cannot always do this.

CHAPTER I.

HOW TO BE HAPPY *THOUGH* MARRIED.

"How delicious is the winning
Of a kiss at love's beginning,
When two mutual hearts are sighing
For the knot there's no untying!"—*T. Campbell.*

"Deceive not thyself by over-expecting happiness in the married state. Look not therein for contentment greater than God will give, or a creature in this world can receive, namely, to be free from all inconveniences. Marriage is not like the hill Olympus, wholly clear, without clouds."—*Fuller.*

"How to be happy *though* married." This was the quaint title of one of Skelton's sermons, which would certainly cause a momentary cloud of indignation, not to say of alarm, to pass over the minds of a newly-married couple, should they discover it when skimming through a collection of old volumes on the first wet day of their honeymoon.

"Two young persons thrown together by chance, or brought together by artifice, exchange glances, reciprocate civilities, and go home to dream of each other. Finding themselves rather uncomfortable apart, they think they necessarily must be happy together." But there is no such necessity. In marriage the measure of our happiness is usually in proportion to our deserts.

"No man e'er gained a happy life by chance,
Or yawned it into being with a wish."

This, however, is just what many novices think they can do in reference to matrimony. They fancy that it has a magic power of conferring happiness almost in spite of themselves, and are quite surprised when experience teaches them that domestic felicity, like everything else worth having, must be worked for—must be earned by patient endurance, self-restraint, and loving consideration for the tastes, and even for the faults, of him or her with whom life is to be lived.

And yet before the first year of married life has ended, most people discover that Skelton's subject, "How to be happy though married," was not an unpractical one. Then they know that the path upon which they have entered may be strewn with thorns instead of with roses, unless mutual forbearance and mutual respect guard the way. The old bachelor who said that marriage was "a very harmless amusement" would not have pronounced such an unconditional judgment had he known more about it. Matrimony is a harmless and a happy state only when careful precaution is taken to defend the domain of the affections from harshness and petulance, and to avoid certain moral and physical pitfalls.

Like government, marriage must be a series of compromises; and however warm the love of both parties may be, it will very soon cool unless they learn the golden rule of married life, "To bear and to forbear." In matrimony, as in so many other things, a good beginning is half the battle. But how easily may good beginnings be frustrated through infirmity of temper and other causes, and then we must "tread those steps with sorrow which we might have trod with joy."

"I often think," says Archdeacon Farrar, "that most of us in life are like many of those sight-seers who saunter through this (Westminster) Abbey. Their listless look upon its grandeur and its memorials furnishes an illustration of the aspect which we present to higher powers as we wander restlessly through the solemn minster-aisles of life.... We talk of human misery; how many of us derive from life one-tenth part of what God meant to be its natural blessedness? Sit out in the open air on a summer day, and how many of us have trained ourselves to notice the sweetness and the multiplicity of the influences which are combining for our delight—the song of birds; the breeze beating balm upon the forehead; the genial warmth; the delicate odour of ten thousand flowers?"

What is said here of life in general is also true of married life. We go through the temple of Hymen without noticing, much less appreciating, its beauty. Certainly few people gain as much happiness from their marriage as they might. They expect to find happiness without taking any trouble to make it, or they are so selfishly preoccupied that they cannot enjoy. In this way many a husband and wife only begin to value each other when death is at hand to separate them.

In married life sacrifices must be ever going on if we would be happy. It is the power to make another glad which lights up our own face with joy. It is the power to bear another's burden which lifts the load from our own heart. To foster with vigilant, self-denying care the development of another's life is the surest way to bring into our own joyous, stimulating energy. Bestow nothing, receive nothing; sow nothing, reap nothing; bear no burden of others, be crushed under your own. If many people are miserable though married, it is because they ignore the great law of self-sacrifice that runs through all nature, and expect blessedness from receiving rather than from giving. They reckon that they have a right to so much service, care, and tenderness from those who love them, instead of asking how much service, care, and tenderness they can give.

No knowledge is so well worth acquiring as the science of living harmoniously for the most part of a life with another, which we might take as a definition of matrimony. This science teaches us to avoid fault-finding, bothering, boring, and other tormenting habits.

"These are only trifling faults," you say. Yes, but trifles produce domestic misery, and domestic misery is no trifle.

"Since trifles make the sum of human things,
And half our misery from those trifles springs,
Oh! let the ungentle spirit learn from thence,
A *small* unkindness is a *great* offence.
To give rich gifts perhaps we wish in vain,
But all may shun the guilt of giving pain."

Husband and wife should burn up in the bonfire of first-love all hobbies and "little ways" that could possibly prevent home from being sweet. How happy people are, though married, when they can say of each other what Mrs. Hare says of her husband in "Memorials of a Quiet Life": "I never saw anybody so easy to live with, by whom the daily petty things of life were passed over so lightly; and then there is a charm in the *refinement* of feeling which is not to be told in its influence upon trifles."

A married pair should be all the world to each other. Sydney Smith's definition of marriage is well known: "It resembles a pair of shears, so joined that they cannot be separated, often moving in opposite directions, yet always punishing any one who comes between them." Certainly those who go between deserve to be punished; and in whatever else they may differ, married people should agree to defend themselves from the well-meant, perhaps, but irritating interference of friends. Above all, they should remember the proverb about the home-washing of soiled linen, for, as old Fuller said, "Jars concealed are half reconciled; while, if generally known, 'tis a double task to stop the breach at home and men's mouths abroad."

Why should love-making end with courtship, and of what use are conquests if they are not guarded? If the love of a life-partner is of far more value than our perverse fancies, it is the part of wisdom to restrain these in order to keep that. A suggestion was recently made from an American pulpit that there was room for a new society which should teach husband and wife their duty to each other. "The first article of the constitution should be that any person applying for membership should solemnly covenant and agree that throughout married life he or she would carefully observe and practise all courtesy, thoughtfulness, and unselfishness that belong to what is known as the 'engagement' period. The second article should be that neither member of a conjugal partnership should listen to a single word of criticism of the other member from any relative whatever, even should the words of wisdom drop from the lips of father, mother, brother, or sister. The rules of the new society need not extend beyond these two, for there would be nothing in the conduct of members in good standing to require other special attention."

The wife, on her part, ought not to be less desirous than she was in the days of courtship of winning her husband's admiration, merely because she now wears upon her finger a golden pledge of his love. Why should she give up those pretty wiles to seem fair and pleasant in his eyes, that were suggested in love-dreams? Instead of lessening her charms, she should endeavour to double them, in order that home may be to him who has paid her the greatest compliment in his power, the dearest and brightest spot upon earth—one to which he may turn for comfort when sick of business and the weary ways of men generally.

George Eliot tells us that marriage must be a relation either of sympathy or of conquest; and it is undoubtedly true that much of the matrimonial discord that exists arises from the mutual struggle for supremacy. They go to church and say "I will," and then, perhaps, on the way home, one or other says "I won't," and that begins it. "What is the reason," said one Irishman to another, "that you and your wife are always disagreeing?" "Because," replied Pat, "we are both of one mind—she wants to be master and so do I." How shall a man retain his wife's affections? Is it by not returning them? Certainly not. The secret of conjugal felicity is contained in this formula: demonstrative affection and self-sacrifice. A man should not only love his wife dearly, but he should tell her that he loves her, and tell her very often, and each should be willing to yield, not once or twice, but constantly, and as a practice to the other. Selfishness crushes out love, and most of the couples who are living without affection for each other, with cold and dead hearts, with ashes where there should be a bright and holy flame, have destroyed themselves by caring too much for themselves and too little for each other.

Each young couple that begins housekeeping on the right basis brings the Garden of Eden before man once more. There are they, two, alone; love raises a wall between them and the outer world. There is no serpent there—and, indeed, he need never come, nor does he, so long as Adam and Eve keep him at bay; but too often the hedge of love is broken, just a little, by small discourtesies, little inattentions, small incivilities, that gradually but surely become wider and wider holes, until there is no hedge at all, and all sorts of monsters enter in and riot there.

"Out of the very ripeness of life's core,
A worm was bred."

The only real preservative against this worm is true religion. Unhappily for themselves the healthy and young sometimes fancy that *they* need not think of this. They forget that religion is required to ennoble and sanctify this present life, and are too liable to associate it exclusively with the contemplation of death. "So 'a cried out—God, God, God! three or four times: now I, to comfort him, bid him 'a should not think of God; I hoped there was no need to trouble himself with any such thoughts yet." This advice, which Mrs. Quickly gave to Falstaff on his deathbed, reflects the thoughts of many people, but it was not sound advice. Certainly it would be cruel rather than kind to advise a young pair who have leaped into the dark of married life not to think of God. He is a Saviour from trouble rather than a troubler, and the husband and wife who never try to serve Him will not be likely to serve each other or to gain much real happiness from their marriage.

The following is related in the memoirs of Mary Somerville. When a girl she and her brother had coaxed their timid mother to accompany them for a sail. The day was sunny, but a stiff breeze was blowing, and presently the boat began to toss and roll. "George," Mrs. Fairfax called to the man in charge, "this is an awful storm! I fear we are in great danger; mind how you steer; remember I trust in you!" He replied, "Dinna trust in me, leddy; trust in God Almighty." In terror the lady exclaimed, "Dear me, is it come to that!" To *that* it ought to come on the day of marriage quite as much as on the day of death. It is not only in times of danger and distress that we want God's presence, but in the time of our well-being, when all goes merry as a marriage bell. Live away from Him, and the happiness you enjoy to-day may become your misery to-morrow.

CHAPTER II.

TO BE OR NOT TO BE—MARRIED?

"A bitter and perplexed 'What shall I do?'"—*Coleridge.*

"Then, why pause with indecision
When bright angels in thy vision
Beckon thee to fields Elysian?"—*Longfellow.*

To be or not to be—married? That is the question that may occur to readers of the last chapter. If so much precaution and preparation are necessary to ensure a harmless, not to say a happy marriage, is the game worth the candle? Is it not better for the unmarried to cultivate the contented state of mind of that old Scotch lady who said, "I wadna gie my single life for a' the double anes I ever saw"?

The controversy as to whether celibacy or wedlock be the happier state is a very old one, perhaps as old as what may be called the previous question—whether life itself be worth living. Some people are very ingenious in making themselves miserable, no matter in what condition of life they find themselves; and there are a sufficient number of querulous celibates as well as over-anxious married people in the world to make us see the wisdom of the sage's words: "Whichever you do, whether you marry or abstain, you will repent." If matrimony has more pleasures and celibacy fewer pains, if loving be "a painful thrill, and not to love more painful still," it is impossible exactly to balance the happiness of these two states, containing respectively more pleasure and more pain, and less pleasure and less pain. "If hopes are dupes, fears may be liars."

It has been said of the state of matrimony that those who are in desire to get out, and those who are out, wish to enter. The more one thinks on the matter in this spirit, the more one becomes convinced that the Scotch minister was by no means an alarmist who thus began an extempore marriage service: "My friends, marriage is a blessing to a few, a curse to many, and a great uncertainty to all. Do ye venture?" After a pause, he repeated with great emphasis, "Do ye venture?" No objection being made to the venture, he then said, "Let's proceed."

With the opinion of this Scotch minister we may compare that of Lord Beaconsfield: "I have often thought that all women should marry, and no men." The Admiral of Castile said, that "he who marries a wife and he who goes to war must necessarily submit to everything that may happen." There will, however, always be young men and maidens who believe that nothing can happen in matrimony that is worse than never to be married at all.

When Joseph Alleine, who was a great student, married, he received a letter of congratulation from an old college friend, who said that he had some thoughts of following his example, but wished to be wary, and would therefore take the freedom of asking him to describe the inconveniences of a married life. Alleine replied, "Thou would'st know the inconveniences of a wife, and I will tell thee. First of all, whereas thou risest constantly at four in the morning, or before, she will keep thee till six; secondly, whereas thou usest to study fourteen hours in the day, she will bring thee to eight or nine; thirdly, whereas thou art wont to forbear one meal at least in the day for thy studies, she will bring thee to thy meat. If these are not mischief enough to affright thee, I know not what thou art." Most people will think that such "inconveniences of a wife" are the strongest arguments in her favour. Nearly all men, but especially bookish men, require the healthy common-sense influence of women to guide and sweetly order their lives. If we make fools of ourselves with them, we are even greater fools without them.

With whatever luxuries a bachelor may be surrounded, he will always find his happiness incomplete unless he has a wife and children to share it.

Who does not sympathize with Leigh Hunt? When in prison he wrote to the governor requesting that "his wife and children might be allowed to be with him in the daytime: that his happiness was bound up in them, and that a separation in respect of abode would be almost as bad to him as tearing his body asunder."

To be, or not to be—married? This is one of those questions in reference to which the speculative reason comes to no certain conclusion. *Solvitur ambulando.* It has nearly distracted some men, whose minds were sicklied o'er with the pale cast of thought. They have almost died of indecision, like the donkey between two exactly similar bundles of hay. An individual of this description, who was well known to the writer, after dropping into a letter-pillar a proposal to a young lady, was seen a few moments afterwards endeavouring to extract with a stick the precious document. Failing in his attempt, the wretched mortal walked round and round the pillar, tortured with the recurrence of reasons against matrimony which he had lately argued away. Fortunately for both parties the lady refused the tempting offer.

And yet this hesitating lover was, perhaps, but a type of many young men of the age. Nowadays, it is often said they are giving up matrimony as if it were some silly old habit suited only to their grandfathers and grandmothers. The complaint is an old one. It was brought against pagan youths more than eighteen hundred years ago, and yet the world has got along. But can all the blame be justly thrown upon the one sex to the exclusion of the other? Have thoughtless extravagance and ignorance of household economy on the part of the ladies no share in deterring the men from making so perilous a venture?

It is said that years ago in Burmah the ladies of the Court met in formal parliament to decide what should be done to cure the increasing aversion of young men to marriage. Their decision was a wise one. They altered, by an order from the palace, the style of dress to be worn by all honest women, reduced the ornaments to be assumed by wives to the fewest and simplest possible, and ordained that at a certain age women should withdraw from the frivolities of fashion and of the fashionable world. Success was the result, and young Burmah went up in a body to the altar.

Robert Burton, in his very quaint and interesting "Anatomy of Melancholy," gives an abstract of all that may be said "to mitigate the miseries of marriage," by Jacobus de Voragine. "Hast thou means? thou hast none to keep and increase it. Hast none? thou hast one to help to get it. Art in prosperity? thine happiness is doubled. Art in adversity? she'll comfort, assist, bear a part of thy burden to make it more tolerable. Art at home? she'll drive away melancholy. Art abroad? she looks after thee going from home, wishes for thee in thine absence, and joyfully welcomes thy return. There's nothing delightsome without society, no society so sweet as matrimony. The band of conjugal love is adamantine. The sweet company of kinsmen increaseth, the number of parents is doubled, of brothers, sisters, nephews. Thou art made a father by a fair and happy issue. Moses curseth the barrenness of matrimony—how much more a single life!" "All this," says Burton, "is true; but how easy a mater is it to answer quite opposite! To exercise myself I will essay. Hast thou means? thou hast one to spend it. Hast none? thy beggary is increased. Art in prosperity? thy happiness is ended. Art in adversity? like Job's wife, she'll aggravate thy misery, vex thy soul, make thy burden intolerable. Art at home? she'll scold thee out of doors. Art abroad? If thou be wise, keep thee so; she'll perhaps graft horns in thine absence, scowl on thee coming home. Nothing gives more content than solitariness, no solitariness like this of a single life. The band of marriage is adamantine—no hope of loosing it; thou art undone. Thy number increaseth; thou shalt be devoured by thy wife's friends. Paul commends marriage, yet he prefers a single life. Is marriage honourable? What an immortal crown belongs to virginity! 'Tis a hazard both ways, I confess, to live single, or to marry; it may be bad, it may be good; as it is a cross and calamity on the one side, so 'tis a sweet delight, an incomparable happiness, a blessed estate, a most unspeakable benefit, a sole content, on the other—'tis all in the proof."

In balancing this question Lord Bacon takes higher ground, and thinks of the effect of marriage and celibacy on a man in his public capacity. "He that hath wife and children hath given hostages to Fortune, for they are impediments to great enterprises, either of virtue or mischief. Certainly the best works, and of the greatest merit for the public, have proceeded from the unmarried or childless men, which, both in affection and means, have married and endowed the public. Yet it were great reason that those that have children should have greatest care of future times, unto which they know they must transmit their dearest pledges. Some there are who, though they lead a single life, yet their thoughts do end with themselves, and account future times impertinences. Nay, there are some other that account wife and children but as bills of charges. Nay more, there are some foolish, rich, covetous men that take a pride in having no children because they may be thought so much the richer. For perhaps they have heard some talk: 'Such an one is a great rich man;' and another except to it: 'Yea, but he hath a great charge of children,' as if it were an abatement to his riches. But the most ordinary cause of a single life is liberty, especially in certain self-pleasing and humorous minds, which are so sensible of every restraint, as they will go near to think their girdles and garters to be bonds and shackles. Unmarried men are best friends, best masters, best servants, but not always best subjects, for they are light to run away, and almost all fugitives are of that condition. A single life doth well with church men, for charity will hardly water the ground where it must first fill a pool."

After all, these enumerations of the comparative advantages of marriage and celibacy are of little use, for a single glance of a pair of bright eyes will cause antimatrimonial arguments to go down like ninepins. The greatest misogamists have been most severely wounded when least expecting it by the darts of Cupid. Such a mishap, according to the anatomist of melancholy already quoted, had "Stratocles the physician, that blear-eyed old man. He was a severe woman's-hater all his life, a bitter persecutor of the whole sex; he foreswore them all still, and mocked them wheresoever he came in such vile terms, that if thou hadst heard him thou wouldst have loathed thine own mother and sisters for his word's sake. Yet this old doting fool was taken at last with that celestial and divine look of Myrilla, the daughter of Anticles the gardener, that smirking wench, that he shaved off his bushy beard, painted his face, curled his hair, wore a laurel crown to cover his bald pate, and for her love besides was ready to run mad."

If it be true that "nothing is certain but death and taxes," we must not seek for mathematical demonstration that the road we propose to travel on is the right one when we come to crossroads in life. A certain amount of probability ought to make us take either one or the other, for not to resolve is to resolve. In reference to such questions as marriage *versus* celibacy, the choice of a wife, the choice of a profession, and many others, there must be a certain venture of faith, and in this unintelligible world there is a rashness which is not always folly.

There are, of course, many persons who, if they married, would be guilty of great imprudence, not to say of downright crime. When, however, two *lovers*—we emphasise the word—have sufficient means, are of a suitable age, and are conscious of no moral, intellectual, or physical impediment, let them marry. It is the advice of some very wise men. Benjamin Franklin wrote to a young friend upon his marriage: "I am glad you are married, and congratulate you most cordially upon it. You are now in the way of becoming a useful citizen, and you have escaped the unnatural state of celibacy for life—the fate of many here who never intended it, but who, having too long postponed the change of their condition, find at length that it is too late to think of it, and so live all their lives in a situation that greatly lessens a man's value. An old volume of a set of books bears not the value of its proportion to the set. What think you of the odd half of a pair of scissors? It can't well cut anything—it may possibly serve to scrape a trencher!"

Dr. Johnson says: "Marriage is the best state for man in general; and every man is a worse man in proportion as he is unfit for the married state." Of marriage Luther observed: "The utmost blessing that God can confer on a man is the possession of a good and pious wife, with whom he may live in peace and tranquillity, to whom he may confide his whole possessions, even his life and welfare." And again he said: "To rise betimes and to marry young are what no man ever repents of doing." Shakespeare would not "admit impediments to the marriage of true minds."

The cares and troubles of married life are many, but are those of single life few? The bachelor has no one on whom in all cases he can rely. As a rule his expenses are as great as those of a married man, his life less useful, and certainly it is less cheerful. "What a life to lead!" exclaims Cobbett. "No one to talk to without going from home, or without getting some one to come to you; no friend to sit and talk to, pleasant evenings to pass! Nobody to share with you your sorrows or your pleasures; no soul having a common interest with you; all around you taking care of themselves and no care of you! Then as to gratifications, from which you will hardly abstain altogether—are they generally of little expense? and are they attended with no trouble, no vexation, no disappointment, no *jealousy* even? and are they never followed by shame and remorse? To me no being in this world appears so wretched as an *old bachelor*. Those circumstances, those changes in his person and in his mind, which in the husband increase rather than diminish the attentions to him, produce all the want of feeling attendant on disgust; and he beholds in the conduct of the mercenary crowd that surround him little besides an eager desire to profit from that event the approach of which nature makes a subject of sorrow with him."

And yet it would be very wrong to hasten young men in this matter, for however miserable an old bachelor may be, he is far more happy than either a bad husband or the husband of a bad wife. What is one man's meat may be another man's poison. To some persons we might say, "If you marry you do well, but if you marry not you do better." In the case of others marriage may have decidedly the advantage. Like most other things marriage is good or bad according to the use or abuse we make of it. The applause that is usually given to persons on entering the matrimonial stage is, to say the least, premature. Let us wait to see how they will play their parts.

And here we must protest against the foolish and cowardly ridicule that is sometimes bestowed upon elderly men and women who, using the liberty of a free country, have abstained from marrying. Certainly some of them could give reasons for spending their lives outside the temple of Hymen that are far more honourable than the motives which induced their foolish detractors to rush in. Some have never found their other selves, or circumstances prevented the junction of these selves. And which is more honourable—a life of loneliness or a loveless marriage? There are others who have laid down their hopes of wedded bliss for the sake of accomplishing some good work, or for the sake of a father, mother, sister, or brother. In such cases celibacy is an honourable and may be a praiseworthy state.

To make "old maid" a term of reproach has mischievous results, and causes many an ill-assorted marriage. Girls have been hurried into marriage by the dread of being so stigmatized who have repented the step to their dying day. The sacredness of marriage and the serious responsibilities it brings are either ignored altogether or but lightly considered when marriage is represented as the only profession for women. There is no truth in Brigham Young's doctrine that only a woman *sealed* to a man in marriage can possibly be saved.

Let mothers teach their daughters that although a well-assorted marriage based upon mutual love and esteem may be the happiest calling for a woman, yet that marriage brings its peculiar trials as well as special joys, and that it is quite possible for a woman to be both useful and happy, although youth be fled, and the crowning joys of life—wife and motherhood—have passed her by or been voluntarily surrendered.

But this fact that celibacy has many consolations need not prevent the conclusion that as a rule married life is to be preferred.

"Jeanie," said an old Cameronian to his daughter, who was asking his permission to marry—"Jeanie, it's a very solemn thing to get married."

"I ken that, father," said the sensible lassie, "but it's a great deal solemner to be single."

Marriages are made in heaven: matrimony in itself is good, but there are fools who turn every blessing into a curse, like the man who said, "This is a good rope, I'll hang myself with it."

CHAPTER III.

MARRIAGE-MADE MEN.

"A wife's a man's best peace, who, till he marries,
Wants making up....
She is the good man's paradise, and the bad's
First step to heaven."—*Shirley.*

"Th' ever womanly
Draweth us onward!"—*Goethe.*

"This is well,
To have a dame indoors, that trims us up,
And keeps us tight."—*Tennyson.*

If there be any *man*—women are seldom anti-matrimonial bigots—who seriously doubts that the *pros* in favour of marriage more than counterbalance the *cons*, we commend to his consideration a few historical instances in which men have been made men in the highest sense of the word by marriage.

We do not endorse the exaggerated statement of Richter that "no man can live piously or die righteously without a wife," but we think that the chances of his doing so are considerably lessened. It is not good for a man to live alone with his evil thoughts. The checks and active duties of marriage are the best antidote, not only to an impure life, but to the dreaming and droning of a useless and purposeless one.

Certainly there are some men and women who without wives or husbands are marriage-made in the sense of having their love and powers drawn out by interesting work. They are married to some art or utility, or instead of loving one they love all. When this last is the case they go down into the haunts of evil, seek out the wretched, and spare neither themselves nor their money in their Christ-like enthusiasm for humanity. But the luxury of doing good is by no means confined to the celibate. On the contrary, the man with a wife and children in whose goodness and happiness he rejoices may be much better prepared to aid and sympathize with the erring and the suffering. The flood-gates of his affections may have been opened, and he may have become receptive to influences which had upon him beforetime little or no effect.

Not a few good and great men have confessed that they were marriage-made to a very considerable extent. The following testimony was given by De Tocqueville in a letter to a friend: "I cannot describe to you the happiness yielded in the long run by the habitual society of a woman, in whose soul all that is good in your own is reflected naturally, and even improved. When I say or do a thing which seems to me to be perfectly right, I read immediately in Marie's countenance an expression of proud satisfaction which elevates me; and so when my conscience reproaches me her face instantly clouds over. Although I have great power over her mind, I see with pleasure that she awes me; and so long as I love her as I do now I am sure that I shall never allow myself to be drawn into anything that is wrong."

Many a man has been shown the pathway to heaven by his wife's practice of piety. "My mercy," says Bunyan, "was to light upon a wife whose father and mother were accounted godly. This woman and I, though we came together as poor as poor might be (not having so much household stuff as a dish or a spoon betwixt us both), yet she had for her part 'The Plain Man's Pathway to Heaven' and 'The Practice of Piety,' which her father had left her when he died." By reading these and other good books, helped by the kindly influence of his wife, Bunyan was gradually reclaimed from his evil ways, and led gently into the way of righteousness.

Nor does this companionship of good wives, which enables men to gain "in sweetness and in moral height," cause them in the least degree to lose "the wrestling thews which throw the world." Quite the reverse. Weak men have displayed real public virtue, and strong men have been made stronger, because they had by their side a woman of noble character, who exercised a fortifying influence on their conduct. Lady Rachel Russell is one of the many celebrated women who have encouraged their husbands to suffer and be strong. She sat beside her husband day after day during his public trial, taking notes and doing everything to help him.

In the sixth year of his marriage Baxter was brought before the magistrates for holding a conventicle, and was sentenced to be confined in Clerkenwell Gaol. There he was joined by his wife, who affectionately nursed him during his imprisonment. "She was never so cheerful a companion to me," he says, "as in prison, and was very much against me seeking to be released."

There is a sort of would-be wit which consists in jesting at the supposed bondage of the married state. The best answer to this plentiful lack of wit is the fact that some of the best of men have kissed the shackles which a wife imposes, and have either thought or said, "If this be slavery, who'd be free?" Luther, speaking of his wife, said, "I would not exchange my poverty with her for all the riches of Crœsus without her." In more recent times the French statesman, M. Guizot, says in his "Mémoires": "What I know to-day, at the end of my race, I have felt when it began, and during its continuance. Even in the midst of great undertakings domestic affections form the basis of life, and the most brilliant career has only superficial and incomplete enjoyments if a stranger to the happy ties of family and friendship." Not long ago, when speaking of his wife, Prince Bismarck said, "She it is who has made me what I am."

And there have been English statesmen who could say quite as much. Burke was sustained amid the anxiety and agitation of public life by domestic felicity. "Every care vanishes," he said, "the moment I enter under my own roof!" Of his wife he said that she was "not made to be the admiration of everybody, but the happiness of one." A writer in a recent number of *Leisure Hour* relates the following of Lord Beaconsfield: "The grateful affection which he entertained for his wife, whom he always esteemed as the founder of his fortunes, is well known. She was in the habit of travelling with him on almost all occasions. A friend of the earl and of the narrator of the incident was dining with him, when one of the party—a Member of the House for many years, of a noble family, but rather remarkable for raising a laugh at his buffoonery than any admiration for his wisdom—had no better taste or grace than to expostulate with Disraeli for always taking the viscountess with him. 'I cannot understand it,' said the graceless man, 'for, you know, you make yourself a perfect laughing-stock wherever your wife goes with you.' Disraeli fixed his eyes upon him very expressively and said, 'I don't suppose you can understand it, B.—I don't suppose you can understand it, for no one could ever in the last and wildest excursions of an insane imagination suppose you to be guilty of gratitude!'"

It is true that there have been memorable celibates, but in the main the world's work has been done by the married. Fame and reward are powerful incentives, but they bear no comparison to the influence exercised by affection.

A man's wife and family often compel him to do his best; and, when on the point of despairing, they force him to fight like a hero, not for himself, but for them. Curran confessed that when he addressed a court for the first time, if he had not felt his wife and children tugging at his gown, he would have thrown up his brief and relinquished the profession of a lawyer.

"It is often the case when you see a great man, like a ship, sailing proudly along the current of renown, that there is a little tug—his wife—whom you cannot see, but who is directing his movements and supplying the motive power." This truth is well illustrated by the anecdote told of Lord Eldon, who, when he had received the Great Seal at the hands of the king, being about to retire, was addressed by his majesty with the words, "Give my remembrance to Lady Eldon." The Chancellor, in acknowledging the condescension, intimated his ignorance of Lady Eldon's claim to such a notice. "Yes, yes," the king answered; "I know how much I owe to Lady Eldon. I know that you would have made yourself a country curate, and that she has made you my Lord Chancellor." Sir Walter Scott and Daniel O'Connell, at a late period of their lives, ascribed their success in the world principally to their wives.

When Sir Joshua Reynolds—himself a bachelor—met the sculptor Flaxman shortly after his marriage, he said to him, "So, Flaxman, I am told you are married; if so, sir, I tell you you are ruined for an artist." Flaxman went home, sat down beside his wife, took her hand in his, and said, "Ann, I am ruined for an artist." "How so, John? How has it happened? and who has done it?" "It happened," he replied, "in the church, and Ann Denman has done it." He then told her of Sir Joshua's remark—whose opinion was well known, and had often been expressed, that if students would excel they must bring the whole powers of their mind to bear upon their art, from the moment they rose until they went to bed; and also, that no man could be a *great* artist unless he studied the grand works of Raphael, Michael Angelo, and others, at Rome and Florence. "And I," said Flaxman, drawing up his little figure to its full height, "*I* would be a great artist." "And a great artist you shall be," said his wife, "and visit Rome, too, if that be really necessary to make you great." "But how?" asked Flaxman. "*Work and economize,*" rejoined the brave wife; "I will never have it said that Ann Denman ruined John Flaxman for an artist." And so it was determined by the pair that the journey to Rome was to be made when their means would admit. "I will go to Rome," said Flaxman, "and show the President that wedlock is for a man's good rather than his harm; and you, Ann, shall accompany me."

After working for five years, aided by the untiring economy of his wife, Flaxman actually did accomplish his journey. On returning from Rome, where he spent seven years, conscious of his indebtedness to his wife, he devised an original gift as a memorial of his domestic happiness. He caused a little quarto book to be made, containing some score or so of leaves, and with pen and pencil proceeded to fill and embellish it. On the first page is drawn a dove with an olive branch in her mouth; an angel is on the right and an angel on the left, and between is written, "To Ann Flaxman"; below, two hands are clasped as at an altar, two cherubs bear a garland, and there follows an inscription to his wife introducing the subject. Instead of finding his genius maimed by his alliance with Ann Denman, this eminent sculptor was ever ready to acknowledge that his subsequent success was in a great part marriage-made.

It was through the eyes of his wife that Huber, the great authority on bees, who was blind from his seventeenth year, conducted his observations and studies. He even went so far as to declare that he should be miserable were he to regain his eyesight. "I should not know," he said, "to what extent a person in my situation could be beloved; besides, to me my wife is always young, fresh, and pretty, which is no light matter."

Sir William Hamilton of Edinburgh found his wife scarcely less helpful, especially after he had been stricken by paralysis through overwork. When he was elected Professor of Logic and Metaphysics, and had no lectures on stock, his wife sat up with him night after night to write out a fair copy of the lectures from the rough sheets which he had drafted in the adjoining room. "The number of pages in her handwriting still preserved is," says Sir William's biographer, "perfectly marvellous."

Equally effective as a literary helper was Lady Napier, the wife of Sir William Napier, historian of the Peninsular War. She translated and epitomized the immense mass of original documents, many of them in cipher, on which it was in a great measure founded. When Wellington was told of the art and industry she had displayed in deciphering King Joseph's portfolios, and the immense mass of correspondence taken at Vittoria, he at first would hardly believe it, adding: "I would have given £20,000 to any person who could have done this for me in the Peninsula." Sir William Napier's handwriting being almost illegible, Lady Napier made out his rough interlined manuscript, which he himself could scarcely read, and wrote out a fair copy for the printer; and all this vast labour she undertook and accomplished, according to the testimony of her husband, without having for a moment neglected the care and education of a large family.

The help and consolation that Hood received from his wife during a life that was a prolonged illness is one of the most affecting things in biography. He had such confidence in her judgment that he read and re-read and corrected with her assistance all that he wrote. He used to trust to her ready memory for references and quotations. Many wives deserve, but few receive, such an I.O.U. as that which the grateful humorist gave to his wife in one of his letters when absent from her side. "I never was anything, Dearest, till I knew you, and I have been a better, happier, and more prosperous man ever since. Lay by that truth in lavender, Sweetest, and remind me of it when I fail. I am writing warmly and fondly, but not without good cause.... Perhaps there is an afterthought that, whatever may befall me, the wife of my bosom will have the acknowledgment of her tenderness, worth, excellence—all that is wifely or womanly—from my pen."

Mr. Froude says of Carlyle's wife that "her hardest work was a delight to her when she could spare her husband's mind an anxiety or his stomach an indigestion. While he was absorbed in his work and extremely irritable as to every ailment or discomfort, her life was devoted to shield him in every possible way." In the inscription upon her tombstone Carlyle bore testimony that he owed to his wife a debt immense of gratitude. "In her bright existence she had more sorrows than are common, but also a soft invincibility, a capacity of discernment, and a noble loyalty of heart which are rare. For forty years she was the true and loving helpmate of her husband, and by act and word unweariedly forwarded him as none else could in all of worthy that he did or attempted. She died at London, April 21st, 1866, suddenly snatched away from him, and the light of his life as if gone out."

What an influence women have exercised upon teachers of religion and philosophy! When no one else would encourage Mahomet, his wife Kadijah listened to him with wonder, with doubt. At length she answered: "Yes, it was true this that he said." We can fancy, as does Carlyle, the boundless gratitude of Mahomet, and how, of all the kindnesses she had done him, this of believing the earnest struggling word he now spoke was the greatest. "It is certain," says Novalis, "my conviction gains infinitely the moment another soul will believe in it." It is a boundless favour. He never forgot this good Kadijah. Long afterwards, Ayesha, his young favourite wife, a woman who indeed distinguished herself among the Moslem by all manner of qualities, through her whole long life, this young brilliant Ayesha was one day questioning him: "Now am I not better than Kadijah? she was a widow; old, and had lost her looks: you love me better than you did her?" "No, by Allah!" answered Mahomet: "No, by Allah! She believed in me when none else would believe. In the whole world I had but one friend, and she was that!"

It will suffice to hint at the scientific value of the little that has been disclosed respecting Madame Clothilde de Vaux in elucidating the position of Auguste Comte as a teacher. Some may think that John Stuart Mill first taught his wife and then admired his own wisdom in her. His own account of the matter is very different, as we learn from the dedication of his essay "On Liberty":

"To the beloved and deplored memory of her who was the inspirer, and in part the author, of all that is best in my writings—the friend and wife whose exalted sense of truth and right was my strongest incitement, and whose approbation was my chief reward—I dedicate this volume. Like all that I have written for many years, it belongs as much to her as to me; but the work as it stands has had, in a very insufficient degree, the inestimable advantage of her revision; some of the most important portions having been reserved for a more careful re-examination, which they are now never destined to receive. Were I but capable of interpreting to the world one-half the great thoughts and noble feelings which are buried in her grave, I should be the medium of a greater benefit to it than is ever likely to arise from anything that I can write, unprompted and unassisted by her all but unrivalled wisdom."

In a speech upon woman's rights, a lady orator is said to have exclaimed, "It is well known that Solomon owed his wisdom to the number of his wives!" This is too much; nevertheless, Sir Samuel Romilly gave the experience of many successful men when he said that there was nothing by which through life he had more profited than by the just observations and the good opinion of his wife.

Most people are acquainted with husbands who have lost almost all self-reliance and self-help because their wives have been only too helpful to them. Trollope and George Eliot faithfully portrayed real life in their stories when they put the reins into the hands of good wives and made them drive the domestic coach, to the immense advantage and comfort of the husbands, who never suspected the real state of the case. No man has so thoroughly as Trollope brought into literature the idea which women have of men—creatures that have to be looked after as grown-up little boys; interesting, piquant, indispensable, but shiftless, headstrong, and at bottom absurd.

But this consciousness which good wives have of the helplessness of husbands renders them all the more valuable in their eyes. Before Weinsberg surrendered to its besiegers, the women of the place asked permission of the captors to remove their valuables. The permission was granted, and shortly after the women were seen issuing from the gates carrying their husbands on their shoulders. Indeed it would be impossible to relate a tenth part of the many ways in which good wives have shown affection for and actively assisted their wedded lords. Knowing this to be the case, we were not surprised to read some time since the following piece of Irish news: "An inquiry was held at Mullingar on Wednesday respecting Mr. H. Smythe's claim of £10,000 as compensation for the loss of his wife, who was shot whilst returning from church. The claim was made under the nineteenth section of the Crime Preservation Act, Ireland." The result of the inquiry we do not know, but for ourselves we think that £10,000 would barely compensate for the loss of a really good article in wives.

Some one told an old bachelor that a friend had gone blind. "Let him marry, then," was the crusty reply; "let him marry, and if that doesn't open his eyes, then his case is indeed hopeless." But this, we must remember, was not the experience of a married man.

A friend was talking to Wordsworth of De Quincey's articles about him. Wordsworth begged him to stop; he hadn't read them, and did not wish to ruffle himself about them. "Well," said the friend, "I'll tell you only one thing he says, and then we'll talk of other things. He says your wife is too good for you." The old poet's dim eyes lighted up, and he started from his chair, crying with enthusiasm, "And that's true! There he's right!" his disgust and contempt visibly moderating. Many a man whose faith in womankind was weak before marriage can a few years afterwards sympathize most fully with this pathetic confession of the old poet.

A Scotch dealer, when exhorting his son to practise honesty on the ground of its being the "best policy," quietly added, "I hae tried *baith*." So is it in reference to matrimony and celibacy. The majority of those who have "tried baith" are of opinion that the former is the best policy.

It would be absurd to assert that the marriage state is free from care and anxiety; but what of that? Is not care and trouble the condition of any and every state of life? He that will avoid trouble must avoid the world. "Marriage," says Dr. Johnson, "is not commonly unhappy, but as life is unhappy." And the summing up, so to speak, of this great authority is well known—"Marriage has many pains, but celibacy no pleasures."

CHAPTER IV.

THE CHOICE OF A WIFE.

"Go, draw aside the curtains, and discover
The several caskets to this noble prince:—
Now make your choice."—*Shakespeare.*

"If, as Plutarch adviseth, one must eat *modium salis*, a bushel of salt, with him before he choose his friend, what care should be had in choosing a wife—his second self! How solicitous should he be to know her qualities and behaviour! and, when he is assured of them, not to prefer birth, fortune, beauty, before bringing up and good conditions."—*Robert Burton.*

Whether a man shall be made or marred by marriage greatly depends upon the choice he makes of a wife. Nothing is better than a good woman, nor anything worse than a bad one. The idea of the great electrician Edison's marrying was first suggested by an intimate friend, who made the point that he needed a mistress to preside over his large house, which was being managed by a housekeeper and several servants. Although a very shy man, he seemed pleased with the proposition, and timidly inquired whom he should marry The friend somewhat testily replied, "Any one;" that a man who had so little sentiment in his soul as to ask such a question ought to be satisfied with anything that wore a petticoat and was decent.

Woe to the man who follows such careless advice as this, and marries "any one," for what was said by the fox to the sick lion might be said with equal truth to Hymen: "I notice that there are many prints of feet entering your cave, but I see no trace of any returning." Before taking the irrevocable step choose well, for your choice though brief is yet endless. And, first, we make the obvious suggestion that it is useless to seek perfection in a wife, even though you may fancy yourself capable of giving an adequate return as did the author of the following advertisement: "Wanted by a Young Gentleman just beginning Housekeeping, a Lady between Eighteen and Twenty-five Years of Age, with a good Education, and a Fortune not less than Five Thousand Pounds; Sound Wind and Limb, Five Feet Four Inches without her shoes; Not Fat, nor yet too lean; Good Set of Teeth; No Pride nor Affectation; Not very Talkative, nor one that is deemed a Scold; but of a Spirit to Resent an Affront; of a Charitable Disposition; not Over-fond of Dress, though always Decent and Clean; that will Entertain her Husband's Friends with Affability and Cheerfulness, and Prefer his Company to Public Diversions and gadding about; one who can keep his secrets, that he may open his Heart to her without reserve on all Occasions; that can extend domestic Expenses with

Economy, as Prosperity advances, without Ostentation; and Retrench them with Cheerfulness, if occasion should require. Any Lady disposed to Matrimony, answering this Description, is desired to direct for Y. Z., at the Baptist's Head Coffee-house, Aldermanbury. *N.B.*—The Gentleman can make adequate Return, and is, in every Respect, deserving a Lady with the above Qualifications."

This reminds us of the old lady who told her steward she wished him to attend a neighbouring fair in order to buy her a cow. She explained to him that it must be young, well-bred, fine in the skin, a strawberry in colour, straight in the back, and not given to breaking through fences when it smelt clover on the other side; above all, it was not to cost more than ten pounds. The steward, who was a Scotchman, and a privileged old servant, bowed his head and replied reverently, "Then, my lady, I think ye had better kneel down and pray for her, for ye'll get her nae other way, I'm thinkin'."

While the possession of a little money is by no means a drawback, those do not well consult their happiness who marry for money alone.

"In many a marriage made for gold,
The bride is bought—and the bridegroom sold."

Though Cupid is said to be blind, he is a better guide than the rules of arithmetic. We have false ideas of happiness. What will make me happy—contented? "Oh, if I were rich, I should be happy!" A gentleman who was enjoying the hospitalities of the great millionaire and king of finance, Rothschild, as he looked at the superb appointments of the mansion, said to his host, "You must be a happy man!" "Happy!" said he, "happy! I happy—happy!" "Aye, happy!" "Let us change the subject." John Jacob Astor of America, was also told that he must be a very happy man, being so rich. "Why," said he, "would you take care of my property for your board and clothes? That's all I get for it." In taking a dowry with a wife "thou losest thy liberty," says an old writer: "she will ride upon thee, domineer as she list, wear the breeches in her oligarchical government, and beggar thee besides."

Better to have a fortune *in* your wife than *with* her. "My wife has made my fortune," said a gentleman of great possessions, "by her thrift, prudence, and cheerfulness, when I was just beginning." "And mine has lost my fortune," answered his companion, bitterly, "by useless extravagance, and repining when I was doing well." The girl who brings to her husband a large dowry may also bring habits of luxury learned in a rich home. She may be almost as incapable of understanding straitened circumstances as was the lady of the court of Louis XVI., who, on hearing of people starving, exclaimed, "Poor creatures! No bread to eat! Then let them eat cakes!"

Nor is it wise to marry for beauty alone: as even the finest landscape, seen daily, becomes monotonous, so does the most beautiful face, unless a beautiful nature shine through it. The beauty of to-day becomes commonplace to-morrow; whereas goodness, displayed through the most ordinary features, is perennially lovely. Moreover, this kind of beauty improves with age, and time ripens rather than destroys it. No man is so much to be pitied as the husband of a "professional beauty." Yet beauty, when it betokens health, or when it is the outward and visible sign of an inward and spiritual grace, is valuable, and has a great power of winning affection.

Above all things do not marry a fool who will shame you and reveal your secrets. For ourselves we do not believe the first part at least of Archbishop Whately's definition of woman: "A creature that does not reason, and that pokes the fire from the top." The wife who does not and cannot make use of reason to overcome the daily difficulties of domestic life, and who can in no sense be called the companion of her husband, is a mate who hinders rather than helps. Sooner or later a household must fall into the hands of its women, and sink or swim according to their capacities. It is hard enough for a man to be married to a bad woman; but for a man who marries a foolish woman there is no hope.

"One must love their friends with all their failings, but it is a great failing to be ill," and therefore unless you are one of those rare men who would never lose patience with a wife always in pain, when choosing you should think more of a healthy hue than of a hectic hue, and far more of good lungs than of a tightly-laced waist "See that she chews her food well, and sets her foot down firmly on the ground when she walks, and you're all right."

As regards the marriageable age of women we may quote the following little conversation: "No woman is worth looking at after thirty," said young Mrs. A., a bride with all the arrogant youthfulness of twenty-one summers. "Quite true, my dear," answered Lady D., a very pretty woman some ten or fifteen years older; "nor worth listening to before."

Please yourself, good sir! only do not marry either a child or an old woman. Certainly a man should marry to obtain a friend and companion rather than a cook and housekeeper; but yet that girl is a prize indeed who has so well prepared herself for the business of wifehood as to be able to keep not only her husband company, but her house in good order. "If that man is to be regarded as a benefactor of his species who makes two stalks of corn to grow where only one grew before, not less is she to be regarded as a public benefactor who economizes and turns to the best practical account the food products of human skill and labour."

Formerly a woman's library was limited to the Bible and a cookery-book. This curriculum has now been considerably extended, and it is everywhere acknowledged that "chemistry enough to keep the pot boiling, and geography enough to know the different rooms in her house," is *not* science enough for women. It is surely not impossible, however, for an intending husband to find a girl who can make her higher education compatible with his comforts, who can when necessary bring her philosophy down to the kitchen. Why should literature unfit women for the everyday business of life? It is not so with men. You see those of the most cultivated minds constantly devoting their time and attention to the most homely objects.

The other day, speaking superficially and uncharitably, a person said of a woman, whom he knew but slightly, "She disappoints me utterly. How could her husband have married her? She is commonplace and stupid." "Yes," said a friend, reflectively, "it is strange. She is not a brilliant woman, she is not even an intellectual one; but there is such a thing as a genius for affection, and she has it. It has been good for her husband that he married her." In the sphere of home the graces of gentleness, of patience, of generosity, are far more valuable than any personal attractions or mental gifts and accomplishments. They contribute more to happiness and are the source of sympathy and spiritual discernment. For does not the woman who can love see more and understand more than the most intellectual woman who has no heart?

A vacancy in the floor sweeping department of a public institution having been advertised, the testimonials to the intellectual and moral eminence of an old woman were overwhelming; but after the election it appeared she had only one arm! Not less unfitted to be a wife is the woman who, with every other qualification, has no genius for affection.

Dress is one of the little things that indicate character. A refined woman will always look neat; but, on the other hand, she will not bedizen and bedeck herself with a view to display. Again, there is no condition of life in which industry in a wife is not necessary to the happiness of a family. A lazy mistress makes lazy servants, and, what is worse, a lazy mother makes lazy children.

"But how," asks Cobbett, "is the purblind lover to ascertain whether she, whose smiles have bereft him of his senses—how is he to judge whether the beloved object will be industrious or lazy?" In answer to this question several outward and visible signs are suggested, such as early rising, a lively, distinct utterance, a quick step, "the labours of the teeth; for these correspond with those of the other members of the body, and with the operations of the mind."

Then we are told of a young man in Philadelphia, who, courting one of three sisters, happened to be on a visit to her, when all the three were present, and when one said to the others, "I *wonder* where *our* needle is." Upon which he withdrew, as soon as was consistent with politeness, resolved never to think more of a girl who possessed a needle only in partnership, and who, it appeared, was not too well informed as to the place where even that share was deposited.

It would be impossible even to allude to every point of character that should be observed in choosing a wife. Frugality, or the power to abstain from unnecessary expenditure, is very important, so is punctuality. As to good temper, it is a most difficult thing to ascertain beforehand; smiles are so easily put on for the *lover's* visits. We know the old conundrum—

why are ladies like bells? Because you never know what metal they are made of until you *ring* them. An ingenuous girl thus alluded to the change that is frequently perceptible after marriage. "Your future husband seems very exacting: he has been stipulating for all sorts of things," said her mother to her. "Never mind, Mamma," said the affectionate girl, who was already dressed for the wedding; "these are his last wishes."

There is, however, one way of roughly guessing the qualifications of a girl for the most responsible position of a wife. Find out the character of her mother, and whether the daughter has been a good one and a good sister. Ask yourself, if you respect as well as admire her, and remember the words of Fichte: "No true and enduring love can exist without esteem; every other draws regret after it, and is unworthy of any noble soul."

Thackeray said of women: "What we (men) want for the most part is a humble, flattering, smiling, child-loving, tea-making being, who laughs at our jokes however old they may be, coaxes and wheedles us in our humours, and fondly lies to us through life." And he says of a wife: "She ought to be able to make your house pleasant to your friends; she ought to attract them to it by her grace. Let it be said of her, 'What an uncommonly nice woman Mrs. Brown is!' Let her be, if not clever, an appreciator of cleverness. Above all, let her have a sense of humour, for a woman without a laugh in her is the greatest bore in existence." It is, we think, only very weak men who would wish their wives to "fondly lie" to them in this way. Better to be occasionally wound up like an eight-day clock by one's wife and made to go right. There is no one who gives such wise and brave advice as a good wife. She is another, a calmer and a better self. The heart of her husband doth safely trust in her, for he knows that when her criticism is most severe it is spoken in love and for his own good. Lord Beaconsfield described his wife as "the most severe of critics, but a perfect wife."

Burns the poet, in speaking of the qualities of a good wife, divided them into ten parts. Four of these he gave to good temper, two to good sense, one to wit, one to beauty—such as a sweet face, eloquent eyes, a fine person, a graceful carriage; and the other two parts he divided amongst the other qualities belonging to or attending on a wife—such as fortune, connections, education (that is, of a higher standard than ordinary), family blood, &c.; but he said, "Divide those two degrees as you please, only remember that all these minor proportions must be expressed by fractions, for there is not any one of them that is entitled to the dignity of an integer."

Let us add the famous advice given by Lord Burleigh to his son: "When it shall please God," said he, "to bring thee to man's estate, use great providence and circumspection in choosing thy wife, for from thence will spring all thy future good or evil. And it is an action of thy life, like unto a stratagem of war, wherein a man can err but once.... Inquire diligently of her disposition, and how her parents have been inclined in their youth. Let her not be poor, how generous (well-born) soever; for a man can buy nothing in the market with gentility. Nor choose a base and uncomely creature altogether for wealth, for it will cause contempt in others, and loathing in thee. Neither make choice of a dwarf or a fool, for by the one thou shalt beget a race of pigmies, while the other will be thy continual disgrace, and it will yirke (irk) thee to hear her talk. For thou shalt find it to thy great grief that there is nothing more fulsome than a she-fool."

The ideal wife is either what Crashaw calls an "impossible she," or—

"Somewhere in the world must be
She that I have prayed to see,
She that Love assigns to me."

But then—

"Shall we ever, ever meet?
Shall I find in thee, my sweet,
Visions true and life complete?"

To the old question, "Who can *find*?" it may too often be replied, Who *seeks* "a virtuous woman"? Is she wealthy? is she pretty? is she talented? are questions asked more frequently than Is she good, sensible, industrious, affectionate? And yet that man takes to himself one of the bitterest of earth's curses who marries carelessly instead of seeking with all diligence for those qualities in a wife that are the foundation of lasting happiness.

A minister's wife falling asleep in church, her husband thus addressed her: "Mrs. B., a' body kens that when I got ye for my wife I got nae beauty; yer frien's ken that I got nae siller; and if I dinna get God's grace I shall hae a puir bargain indeed." If men would seek for wives women with the grace of God, if they would choose them as they do their clothes, for qualities that will last, they would get much better bargains.

One reason for this carelessness about the character of a wife may be found in the prevailing opinion that there is little or no room for choice in matters matrimonial. Sir John More (father of the Chancellor, Sir Thomas) was often heard to say, "I would compare the multitude of women which are to be chosen for wives unto a bag full of snakes, having among them a single eel. Now, if a man should put his hand into this bag, he may chance to light on the eel; but it is a hundred to one he shall be stung by a snake."

Perhaps the lottery theory of marriage was never stated more strongly or with greater cynicism; but is it true? If it were, to expend care and attention in choosing a wife would be to labour in vain. If, however, marriage is by no means such an affair of chance, a prudent choice may prevent a man from being stung by a snake, and may give him a goodly eel as his marriage portion. The important thing to do is to keep well in mind the fact that a man's prospect of domestic felicity does not depend upon the face, the fortune, or the accomplishments of his wife, but upon her character. The son of Sirach says that he would rather dwell with a lion and a dragon than to keep house with a wicked woman. "He that hath hold of her is as though he held a scorpion. A loud crying woman and a scold shall be sought out to drive away the enemies." On the other hand, "the grace of a wife delighteth her husband, and her discretion will fatten his bones. A silent and loving woman is a gift of the Lord; and there is nothing so much worth as a mind well instructed."

CHAPTER V

THE CHOICE OF A HUSBAND.

"How shall I know if I do choose the right?"—*Shakespeare.*

"God, the best maker of marriages, bless you!"—*Ibid.*

"And while thou livest, dear Kate, take a fellow of plain and uncoined constancy; for he perforce must do thee right, because he hath not the gift to woo in other places; for these fellows of infinite tongue, that can rhyme themselves into ladies' favours, they do always reason themselves out again. What! a speaker is but a prater; a rhyme is but a ballad. A good leg will fall; a straight back will stoop; a black beard will turn white; a curled pate will grow bald; a fair face will wither; a full eye will wax hollow; but a good heart, Kate, is the sun and the moon; or, rather, the sun, and not the moon; for it shines bright, and never changes, but keeps his course truly."—*Ibid.*

They that enter into the state of marriage cast a die of the greatest contingency, and yet of the greatest interest in the world, next to the last throw for eternity. Life or death, felicity or a lasting sorrow, are in the power of marriage. A woman, indeed, ventures most, for she hath no sanctuary to retire to from an evil husband; she must dwell upon her sorrow and hatch the eggs which her own folly or infelicity hath produced; and she is more under it, because her tormentor hath a warrant of prerogative, and the woman may complain to God, as subjects do of tyrant princes; but otherwise she hath no appeal in the causes of unkindness. And though the man can run from many hours of his sadness, yet he must return to it again; and when he sits among his neighbours he remembers the objection that is in his bosom, and he sighs deeply. "The boys and the pedlars and the fruiterers shall tell of this man when he is carried to his grave that he lived and died a poor, wretched person."

In these words Jeremy Taylor puts before men and women the issues of choice in matrimony. What, however, concerns us in this chapter is that "a woman ventures most." "Love is of man's life a thing apart, 'tis woman's whole existence." How important that a treasure which is dear as life itself should be placed in safe keeping! And yet so blind is love that defects often seem to be virtues, deformity assumes the style of beauty, and even hideous vices have appeared under an attractive form.

In Shakespeare's play Cleopatra speaks of an old attachment which she had lived to despise as having arisen in her "salad days," when she was green in judgment. In extreme youth love is especially blind, and for this, as well as for other reasons, girls, who are yet at school, do not consult their best interests when they allow love to occupy their too youthful minds. It prevents the enjoyment of happy years of maidenhood, and sometimes leads to marriage before the girl is fit, either physically, mentally, or domestically, for the cares of married life.

"I believe," says R. W. Dale, of Birmingham, "in falling in love. The imagination should be kindled and the heart touched; there should be enthusiasm and even romance in the happy months that precede marriage, and something of the enthusiasm and romance should remain to the very end of life, or else the home is wanting in its perfect happiness and grace. But take my word for it, solid virtues are indispensable to the security and happiness of a home."

You would not like to live with a liar, with a thief, with a drunkard, for twenty or thirty years. A lazy man will make but a weak band or support for his and your house; so will one deficient in fortitude—that is, the power to bear pain and trouble without whining. Beware of the selfish man, for though he may be drawn out of selfishness in the early weeks of courtship, he will settle back into it again when the wear and worry of life come on. And remember that a man may have the roots of some of these vices in him and yet be extremely agreeable and good-looking, dress well, and say very pretty and charming things. "How easy is it for the proper-false in women's waxen hearts to set their forms!"

In their haste to be married many women are too easily satisfied with the characters of men who may offer themselves as husbands. They aim at matrimony in the abstract; not *the* man, but any man. They would not engage a servant if all they knew of her were that she had, as a housemaid lately advertised, "a fortnight's character from her last place;" but with even less information as to their characters they will accept husbands and vow to love, honour, and obey them! In comparison how much more honourable and how much less unloved and unloving is the spinster's lot! Women marry simply for a home because they have not been trained to fight the battle of life for themselves, and because their lives are so dull and stagnant that they think any change must be for the better.

A friend—let us say Barlow—was describing to Jerrold the story of his courtship and marriage: how his wife had been brought up in a convent, and was on the point of taking the veil, when his presence burst upon her enraptured sight. Jerrold listened to the end of the story, and by way of comment said, "Ah! she evidently thought Barlow better than nun." When girls have been given work in the world they do not think that any husband is better than none, and they have not time to imagine themselves in love with the first man who proposes. How often is it the case that people think themselves in love when in fact they are only idle!

There are hearts all the better for keeping; they become mellower and more worth a woman's acceptance than the crude, unripe things that are sometimes gathered—as children gather green fruit—to the discomfort of those who obtain them. A husband may be too young to properly appreciate and take care of a wife. And yet perhaps the majority of girls would rather be a young man's slave than an old man's darling. "My dear," said a father to his daughter, "I intend that you should be married, but not that you should throw yourself away on any wild, worthless boy: you must marry a man of sober and mature age. What do you think of a fine, intelligent husband of fifty?" "I think two of twenty-five would be better, papa."

Prophecies as to the probable result of a marriage are as a rule little to be trusted. It was so in the case of the celebrated Madame Necker. She had been taken to Paris to live with a young widow, to whom Necker—a financier from Geneva—came to pay his addresses. The story goes that the widow, in order to rid herself of her admirer, got him to transfer his addresses to her young companion, saying to herself, "they will bore each other to death, that will give them something to do." The happy pair, however, had no such foreboding. "I am marrying a man," wrote the lady, "whom I should believe to be an angel, if his great love for me did not show his weakness." In his way the husband was equally satisfied. "I account myself as happy as it is possible for a man to be," he wrote to a mutual friend; and to the end of the chapter there was no flaw in that matrimonial life.

Never to marry a genius was the advice of Mrs. Carlyle. "I married for ambition. Carlyle has exceeded all that my wildest hopes ever imagined of him, and I am miserable." As the supply of geniuses is very limited, this advice may seem superfluous. It is not so, however, for there is enough and to spare of men who think that they are geniuses, and take liberties accordingly. These are very often only sons of fond but foolish mothers, who have persuaded them that they are not made of common clay, and that the girls who get them will be blessed. From such a blessing young women should pray to be delivered.

Perhaps it may be said that though it is easy to write about choosing a husband, for the majority of English girls, at least, there is but little choice in the matter. Dickens certainly told an American story—very American—of a young lady on a voyage, who, being intensely loved by five young men, was advised to "jump overboard and marry the man who jumped in after her." Accordingly, next morning the five lovers being on deck, and looking very devotedly at the young lady, she plunged into the sea. Four of the lovers immediately jumped in after her. When the young lady and four lovers were out again, she said to the captain, "What am I to do with them now, they are so wet?" "Take the dry one." And the young lady did, and married him. How different is the state of affairs on this side of the Atlantic, where, if a young woman is to be married, she must take not whom she will, but whom she can. "Oh me, the word choose! I may neither choose whom I would, nor refuse whom I dislike." But is it necessary to marry? Far better to have no husband than a bad one.

There is a great deal of human nature in the account which Artemus Ward gives of the many affecting ties which made him hanker after Betsy Jane. "Her father's farm jined our'n; their cows and our'n squencht their thurst at the same spring; our old mares both had stars in their forrerds; the measles broke out in both famerlies at nearly the same period; our parients (Betsy's and mine) slept reglarly every Sunday in the same meetin-house, and the nabers used to obsarve, 'How thick the Wards and Peasleys air!' It was a surblime site, in the spring of the year, to see our sevral mothers (Betsy's and mine) with their gowns pin'd up so thay couldn't sile 'em affecshunitly bilin sope together and aboozin the nabers."

In this matter more than in most others "we do not will according to our reason, we reason according to our will." True desire, the monition of nature, is much to be attended to. But always we are to discriminate carefully between *true* desire and false. The medical men tell us we should eat what we *truly* have an appetite for; but what we only *falsely* have an appetite for we should resolutely avoid. Ought not choice in matrimony to be guided by the same principle?

Above all things young ladies should ask God, the best maker of marriages, to direct their choice aright.

CHAPTER VI.

ON MAKING THE BEST OF A BAD MATRIMONIAL BARGAIN.

"How poor are they who have not patience!
What wound did ever heal, but by degrees?"—*Shakespeare.*

"E'en now, in passing through the garden walks,
Upon the ground I saw a fallen nest,
Ruined and full of ruin; and over it,
Behold, the uncomplaining birds, already
Busy in building a new habitation."—*Longfellow.*

But "the best laid schemes of mice and men gang aft a-gley." We are none of us infallible, "not even the youngest." When the greatest care has been taken in choosing, people get bad matrimonial bargains. From the nature of the case this must often happen. If not one man in a thousand is a judge of the points of a horse, not one in a million understands human nature. And even if a young man or woman did understand human nature, there are before marriage, as a rule, opportunities of gaining only the slightest knowledge of the character of one who is to be the weal or woe of a new home. It is related in ancient history, or fable, that when Rhodope, a fashionable Egyptian beauty, was engaged bathing, an eagle stole away one of her shoes, and let it fall near Psammetichus the king. Struck with the pretty shoe, he fell in love with the foot, and finally married the owner of both. Very little more acquaintance with each other have the majority of the Innocents who go abroad into the unknown country of Matrimony to seek their fortunes or misfortunes.

And then the temper and manner of people when making love are so different from what these become afterwards! "One would think the whole endeavour of both parties during the time of courtship is to hinder themselves from being known—to disguise their natural temper and real desires in hypocritical imitation, studied compliance, and continued affectation. From the time that their love is avowed, neither sees the other but in a mask; and the cheat is often managed on both sides with so much art, and discovered afterwards with so much abruptness, that each has reason to suspect that some transformation has happened on the wedding-night, and that by a strange imposture, as in the case of Jacob, one has been courted and another married."

Our conventional state of society curtails the limits of choice in matrimony and hinders the natural law of the marriage of the fittest. We knew a young gentleman living in a London suburb who bore an excellent character, had sufficient income, and was in every respect marriageable. He wished to try the experiment of two against the world, but—as he told the clergyman of his parish—he was in the city all day, and never had an opportunity of becoming acquainted with a young lady whom he could ask to be his wife.

We have heard of the stiff Englishman who would not attempt to save a fellow-creature from drowning because he had never been introduced to him. In the same way unmarried ladies are allowed to remain in the Slough of Despond because the valiant young gentlemen who would rescue them, though they may be almost, are not altogether in their social set.

Every one knows Plato's theory about marriage. He taught that men and women were hemispheres, so to speak, of an original sphere; that ill-assorted marriages were the result of the wrong hemispheres getting together; that, if the true halves met, the man became complete, and the consequence was the "happy-ever-after" of childhood's stories. There is much truth in this doctrine, that for every man there is *one* woman somewhere in the world, and for every woman *one* man. They seldom meet in time. If they did, what would become of the sensational novelists?

But are there not in reality too many artificial obstacles to happy marriages? Why do the right men and women so seldom meet? Because mammon, ambition, envy, hatred, and all uncharitableness step between and keep apart those whom God would join together.

It is true that newly-married people when going through the process of being disillusioned are liable to conclude much too quickly that they have got bad matrimonial bargains. In a letter which Mrs. Thrale, the friend of Dr. Johnson, wrote to a young gentleman on his marriage, she says: "When your present violence of passion subsides, and a more cool and tranquil affection takes its place, be not hasty to censure yourself as indifferent, or to lament yourself as unhappy. You have lost that only which it was impossible to retain; and it were graceless amid the pleasures of a prosperous summer to regret the blossoms of a transient spring. Neither unwarily condemn your bride's insipidity, till you have reflected that no object however sublime, no sounds however charming, can continue to transport us with delight, when they no longer strike us with novelty."

Satiety follows quickly upon the heels of possession. A little boy of four years of age told me the other day that he wished to die. "Why?" "Oh, just for a change!" There are children of a larger growth who require continual change and variety to keep them interested.

We expect too much from life in general, and from married life in particular. When castle-building before marriage we imagine a condition never experienced on this side of heaven; and when real life comes with its troubles and cares, the tower of romance falls with a crash, leaving us in the mud-hut of every-day reality. Better to enter the marriage state in the frame of mind of that company of American settlers, who, in naming their new town, called it Dictionary, "because," as they said, "that's the only place where peace, prosperity, and happiness are always to be found."

It would be contrary to the nature of constitutional grumblers to be satisfied with their matrimonial bargains, no matter how much too good for them they may be. They don't want to be satisfied in this or in any other respect, for, as the Irishman said, they are never happy unless they are miserable. They may have drawn a prize in the matrimonial lottery, but they grumble if it be not the highest prize. They are cursed with dispositions like that of the Jew, who, very early one morning, picked up a roll of bank-notes on Newmarket Heath, which had been dropped by some inebriated betting-man the night before. "What have you got there?" exclaimed a fellow Israelite. "Lucky as usual!" "Lucky you call it?" grumbled the man in reply, rapidly turning over the notes. "Lucky is it! all fivers—not a tenner among them!"

Even a perfect matrimonial bargain would not please some people. They are as prone to grumble as the poor woman who, being asked if she were satisfied when a pure water supply had been introduced into Edinburgh, said: "Aye, not so well as I might; it's not like the water we had before—it neither smells nor tastes."

There is a story told of a rustic swain who, when asked whether he would take his partner to be his wedded wife, replied, with shameful indecision, "Yes, I'm willin'; but I'd a much sight rather have her sister." The sort of people who are represented by this vacillating bridegroom are no sooner married than they begin to cast fond, lingering looks behind upon the state of single blessedness they have abandoned, or else upon some lost ideal which they prefer to the living, breathing reality of which they have become possessed. They don't know, and never did know, their own minds.

Let us suppose, however, that a bad matrimonial bargain has been obtained, not in imagination, but in sad earnest—How is the best to be made of it? We must do as Old Mother Hubbard did when she found the cupboard empty—"accept the inevitable with calm steadfastness." It may even be politic to dissemble a little, and pretend we rather enjoy it than otherwise. Above all, do not appeal to the girl's friends for comfort or consolation. They will only laugh at you. Take warning from the unfortunate young man who, every time he met the father of his wife, complained to him of the bad temper and disposition of his daughter. At last, upon one occasion, the old gentleman, becoming weary of the grumbling of his son-in-law, exclaimed: "You are right, sir; she is an impertinent jade; and if I hear any more complaints of her I will disinherit her."

A writer in *Chambers' Journal* gives some instances of matrimonial tribulation that were brought to light in the last census returns. Several husbands returned their wives as the heads of the families; and one described himself as an idiot for having married his literal better-half. "Married, and I'm heartily sorry for it," was returned in two cases; and in quite a number of instances "Temper" was entered under the head of infirmities opposite the name of the wife.

Confessions of this sort, besides being, as we have already hinted, somewhat indiscreet, are often also supererogatory; for conjugal dissension, like murder, will out; and that sometimes in the most provoking and untimely manner. It would be much better to call in the assistance of proper pride than to whine in this cowardly fashion. "We mortals," says George Eliot, "men and women, devour many a disappointment between breakfast and dinner time; keep back the tears and look a little pale about the lips, and in answer to inquiries say, 'Oh, nothing!' Pride helps us; and pride is not a bad thing when it only urges us to hide our own hurts—not to hurt others." "To feel the chains, but take especial care the world shall not hear them clank. 'Tis a prudence that often passes for happiness. It is one of the decencies of matrimony."

"Biddy," said Dean Swift one day to his cook, "this leg of mutton is over-done; take it down and do it less." "Plaze, your Riverence," replied Biddy, "the thing is impossible." "Well, then," rejoined her master, "let this be a lesson to you, that if you must commit mistakes they, at all events, shall not be of such gravity as to preclude correction." Well would it be if people never made mistakes that preclude correction in reference to more important matters! Yet, for all this, it is a good thing that we have no "fatal facility" of divorce in this country, and that a marriage once made is generally regarded as a world-without-end bargain.

A story has been told of a graceless scamp who gained access to the Clarendon printing-office in Oxford, when a new edition of the Prayer-book was ready for the press. In that part of the "forme" already set up which contained the marriage service, he substituted the letter *k* for the letter *v* in the word live; and thus the vow "to love, honour, comfort, &c., so long as ye both shall live," was made to read "so long as ye both shall like!" The change was not discovered until the whole of the edition was printed off. If the sheets are still preserved it would be a good speculation to send them to some of the States in America, where people are "exceedingly divorced." May they long remain useless in Great Britain! For nothing is more dangerous than to unite two persons so closely in all their interests and concerns as man and wife, without rendering the union entire and total.

In that very interesting Bible story of Nabal and Abigail, a noble woman is seen making the best of an extremely bad matrimonial bargain. If her marriage with Nabal, who was a churlish, ill-tempered, drunken fool, was one of the worst possible, does not her conduct teach the lesson that something may be done to mitigate the miseries of even the most frightful state of marriage? Who shall say how many heroines unknown to fame there are who imitate her? Their husbands are weak-willed, foolish, idle, extravagant, dissipated, and generally ne'er-do-weel; but instead of helplessly sitting down to regret their marriage-day, they take the management of everything into their own hands, and make the best of the inevitable by patient endurance in well-doing. It is sometimes said that "any husband is better than none." Perhaps so; in the sense of his being a sort of domestic Attila, a "scourge of God" to "whip the offending Adam" out of a woman and turn her into an angel, as the wives of some bad husbands seem to become.

"I will do anything," says Portia, in the "Merchant of Venice," "ere I will be married to a sponge;" and in answer to the question—"How like you the young German, the Duke of Saxony's nephew?" she answers: "Very vilely in the morning, when he is sober; and most vilely in the afternoon, when he is drunk: when he is best he is a little worse than a man; and when he is worst he is little better than a beast: an the worst fall that ever fell, I hope I shall make shift to go without him."

When a poor girl has not had Portia's discernment to discover such faults before marriage, what can she do? She can do her best.

"What knowest thou, O wife, whether thou shalt save thy husband?" Endeavouring to do this, you will not only have the answer of a good conscience, but will have taken the best precaution against falling yourself, so that it never can be truly said of you—

"As the husband is, the wife is; thou art mated with a clown,
And the grossness of his nature will have weight to drag thee down."

It has been said that to have loved and lost—either by that total disenchantment which leaves compassion as the sole substitute for love which can exist no more, or by the slow torment which is obliged to let go day by day all that constitutes the diviner part of love, namely, reverence, belief, and trust, yet clings desperately to the only thing left it, a long-suffering apologetic tenderness—this lot is probably the hardest any woman can have to bear.

"What is good for a bootless bane?—
And she made answer, 'Endless sorrow.'"

This answer should never have been made, for none but the guilty can be long and completely miserable. The effect and duration of sorrow greatly depends upon ourselves. "If thou hast a bundle of thorns in thy lot, at least thou need'st not insist on sitting down on them." Nor must we forget that there is a "wondrous alchemy in time and the power of God" to transmute our sorrows, as well as our faults and errors, into golden blessings.

It is an old maxim that if one will not, two cannot quarrel. If one of the heads of a house has a bad temper, there is all the more reason for the other to be cool and collected, and capable of keeping domestic peace. Think of Socrates, who, when his wife Zanthippe concluded a fit of scolding by throwing at him a bucket of water, quietly remarked, "After the thunder comes the rain." And when she struck him, to some friends who would have had him strike her again, he replied, that he would not make them sport, nor that they should stand by and say, "*Eia Socrates, eia Zanthippe!*" as boys do when dogs fight, animate them more by clapping hands.

If we would learn how to make the worst instead of the best of a matrimonial bargain, Adam, the first husband, will teach us. He allowed himself to be tempted by Eve, and then like a true coward tried to put all the blame upon her. This little bit of history repeats itself every day. "In the state of innocency Adam fell; and what should poor Jack Falstaff do in the days of villainy?"

There is another way in which people make the worst instead of the best of their bad matrimonial bargains. "Faults are thick where love is thin," and love having become thin they exaggerate the badness of their bargains. A man, having one well-formed and one crooked leg, was wont to test the disposition of his friends, by observing which leg they looked at first or most. Surely the last people we should draw with their worst leg foremost are our life partners. The best of men are only *men* at the best. They are, as Sterne said, "a strange compound of contradictory qualities; and were the accidental oversights and folly of the wisest man—the failings and imperfections of a religious man—the hasty acts and passionate words of a meek man—were they to rise up in judgment against them, and an ill-natured judge to be suffered to mark in this manner what has been done amiss, what character so unexceptionable as to be able to stand before him?" Ought husbands and wives to be ill-natured judges of what is amiss?

"Let a man," says Seneca, "consider his own vices, reflect upon his own follies, and he will see that he has the greatest reason to be angry with himself." The best advice to give husband and wife is to ask them to resolve in the words of Shakespeare, "I will chide no breather in the world but myself, against whom I know most faults." Why beholdest thou the mote that is in the eye of thy matrimonial bargain, but considerest not the beam that is in thine own eye?

When you find yourself complaining of your matrimonial bargain, think sometimes whether you deserve a better one. What right and title has thy greedy soul to domestic happiness or to any other kind of happiness? "Fancy," says Carlyle, "thou deservest to be hanged (as is most likely), thou wilt feel it happiness to be only shot." We may imagine that we deserve a perfect matrimonial bargain, but a less partial observer like Lord Braxfield might make a correction in our estimate. This Scotch judge once said to an eloquent culprit at the bar, "Ye're a verra clever chiel, mon, but I'm thinkin' ye wad be nane the waur o' a hangin'." Equally instructive is the story of a magistrate, who, when a thief remonstrated, "But, sir, I must live," replied, "I don't recognize the necessity." It is only when we cease to believe that we must have supreme domestic and other kinds of felicity, that we are able with a contented mind to bear our share of the "weary weight of all this unintelligible world."

In reference to marriage and to everything else in life, we should sometimes reflect how much worse off we might be instead of how much better. Perhaps you are like the man who said, "I must put up with it," when he had only turkey and plum pudding for dinner. If, as it has often been said, all men brought their grievances of mind, body, and estate—their lunacies, epilepsies, cancers, bereavement, beggary, imprisonment—and laid them on a heap to be equally divided, would you share alike and take your portion, or be as you are? Without question you would be as you are. And perhaps if all matrimonial bargains were to be again distributed, it would be better for you to keep what you have than to run the chance of getting worse. A man who grumbled at the badness of his shoes felt ashamed on meeting with one who had no feet. "Consider the pains which martyrs have endured, and think how even now many people are bearing afflictions beyond all measure greater than yours, and say, 'Of a truth my trouble is comfort, my torments are but roses as compared to those whose life is a continual death, without solace, or aid, or consolation, borne down with a weight of grief tenfold greater than mine.'"

"Oft in life's stillest shade reclining,
In desolation unrepining,
Without a hope on earth to find
A mirror in an answering mind,
Meek souls there are, who little dream
Their daily strife an angel's theme,
Or that the rod they take so calm
Shall prove in Heaven a martyr's palm."

One of these "meek souls" is reported to have said to a friend, "You know not the joy of an accepted sorrow." And of every disappointment, we may truly say that people know not how well it may be borne until they have tried to bear it. This, which is true of disappointment in general, is no less true of the disappointments of a married pair. Those who have not found in marriage all that they fondly, and perhaps over sanguinely, anticipated, may, after some time, become to a certain extent happy though married, if they resolve to do their best under the circumstances.

CHAPTER VII.

MARRIAGE CONSIDERED AS A DISCIPLINE OF CHARACTER.

"Certainly wife and children are a kind of Discipline of Humanity."—*Bacon.*

"I well remember the bright assenting laugh which she (Mrs. Carlyle) once responded to some words of mine, when the propriety was being discussed of relaxing the marriage laws. I had said that the true way to look at marriage was as a discipline of character."—*Froude.*

"Did you ever see anything so absurd as a horse sprawling like that?" This was the hasty exclamation of a connoisseur on taking up a small cabinet picture. "Excuse me," replied the owner, "you hold it the wrong way: it is a horse galloping." So much depends upon the way we look at things. In the preceding chapter we spoke of making the best of bad matrimonial bargains. Perhaps it would help some people to do this if they looked at marriage from a different point of view—if they considered it as a discipline of character rather than as a short cut to the highest heaven of happiness. Certainly this is a practical point of view, and it may be that those who marry in this spirit are more likely to use their matrimony rightly than those who start with happiness as their only goal. That people get happiness by being willing to pass it by and do without it rather than by directly pursuing it, is as true of domestic felicity as of other kinds.

"Ven you're a married man, Samivel," says Mr. Weller to his son Sam, "you'll understand a good many things as you don't understand now; but vether it's worth while going through so much to learn so little, as the charity boy said ven he got to the end of the alphabet, is a matter o' taste: I rayther think it isn't." Strange that a philosopher of the senior Mr. Weller's profundity should underestimate in this way the value of matrimony as a teacher. We have it on the authority of a widower who was thrice married, that his first wife cured his romance, the second taught him humility, and the third made him a philosopher. Another veteran believes that five or six years of married life will often reduce a naturally irascible man to so angelic a condition that it would hardly be safe to trust him with a pair of wings.

Webster asks—

"What do you think of marriage?
I think, as those do who deny purgatory,
It locally contains either heaven or hell,
There is no third place in it."

Is this true? We think not, for we know many married people who live in a third place, the existence of which is here denied. They are neither intensely happy nor intensely miserable; but they lose many faults, and are greatly developed in character by passing through a purgatorial existence. Nor is this an argument against matrimony, except to those who deny that "it is better to be seven times in the furnace than to come out unpurified."

Sweet are the uses of this and every other adversity when these words of Sir Arthur Helps are applicable to its victims or rather victors: "That man is very strong and powerful who has no more hopes for himself, who looks not to be loved any more, to be admired any more, to have any more honour or dignity, and who cares not for gratitude; but whose sole thought is for others, and who only lives on for them."

The young husband may imagine that he only takes a wife to add to his own felicity; taking no account of the possibility of meeting a disposition and temper which may, without caution, mar and blight his own. Women are not angels, although in their ministrations they make a near approach to them. Women, no more than men, are free from human infirmities; the newly-married man must therefore calculate upon the necessity of amendment in his wife as well as of that necessity in himself. The process, however, as well as the result of the process, will yield a rich reward. At a minister's festival meeting "Our Wives" was one of the toasts. One of the brethren, whose wife had a temper of her own, on being sportively asked if he would drink it, exclaimed, "Aye, heartily; Mine brings me to my knees in prayer a dizzen times a day, an' nane o' you can say the same o' yours."

If even bad matrimonial bargains have so much influence in disciplining character, how much more may be learned from a happy marriage! Without it a man or woman is "Scarce half made up." The enjoyments of celibacy, whatever they may be, are narrow in their range, and belong to only a portion of our nature; and whatever the excellences of the bachelor's character, he can never attain to a perfected manhood so long as such a large and important part of his nature as the affections for the gratification of which marriage provides, is unexercised and undeveloped. There are in his nature latent capabilities, both of enjoyment and affection, which find no expression. He is lacking in moral symmetry. The motives from which he keeps himself free from marriage responsibilities may be worthy of the highest respect, but this does not hinder his character from being less disciplined than it might have been.

"For indeed I know
Of no more subtle master under heaven
Than is the maiden passion for a maid,
Not only to keep down the base in man,
But teach high thoughts and amiable words,
And love of truth, and all that makes a man."

On both sides marriage brings into play some of the purest and loftiest feelings of which our nature is capable. The feeling of identity of interest implied in the marriage relation—the mutual confidence which is the natural result—the tender, chivalrous regard of the husband for his wife as one who has given herself to him—the devotion and respect of the wife for the husband as one to whom she has given herself—their mutual love attracted first by the qualities seen or imagined by each in the other, and afterwards strengthened by the consciousness of being that object's best beloved—these feelings exert a purifying, refining, elevating influence, and are more akin to the religious than any other feelings. Love, like all things here, is education. It renders us wise by expanding the soul and stimulating the mental powers.

"Yes, love indeed is light from heaven:
A spark of that immortal fire
With angels shared, by Allah given,
To lift from earth our low desire.
Devotion wafts the mind above,
But heaven itself descends in love;
A feeling from the Godhead caught,
To wean from self each sordid thought;
A ray of Him who formed the whole;
A glory circling round the soul!"

It has been well said, "The first condition of human goodness is something to love; the second, something to reverence." Both these conditions meet in a well-chosen alliance.

Married people may so abuse matrimony as to make it a very school for scandal; but it may and ought to be what Sir Thomas More's home was said to be, "a school and exercise of the Christian religion." "No wrangling, no angry word, was heard in it; no one was idle; every one did his duty with alacrity and not without a temperate cheerfulness." This atmosphere of love and duty which pervaded his home must have been owing in a great measure to the household goodness of Sir Thomas himself. For though his first wife was all that he could have desired, his second was ill-tempered and little capable of appreciating the lofty principles that actuated her husband. "I have lived—I have laboured—I have loved. I have lived in them I loved, laboured for them I loved, loved them for whom I laboured." Well might Sir Thomas add after this reflection, "My labour hath not been in vain;" for to say nothing of its effect upon others, how it must have disciplined his own character!

"There is nothing," you say, "in the drudgery of domestic life to soften." No; but, as Robertson of Brighton says, "a great deal to strengthen with the sense of duty done, self-control, and power. Besides you cannot calculate how much corroding rust is kept off, how much of disconsolate, dull despondency is hindered. Daily use is not the jeweller's mercurial polish, but it will keep your little silver pencil from tarnishing."

"Family life," says Sainte-Beuve, "may be full of thorns and cares; but they are fruitful: all others are dry thorns." And again: "If a man's home at a certain period of life does not contain children, it will probably be found filled with follies or with vices."

Even if it were a misfortune to be married, which we emphatically deny, has not the old Roman moralist taught us that, "to escape misfortune is to want instruction, and that to live at ease is to live in ignorance"? Misfortune to be married? Rather not.

"Life with all it yields of joy and woe
And hope and fear....
Is just our chance o' the prize of the learning love—
How love might be, hath been indeed, and is."

CHAPTER VIII.

BEING MARRIED.

> "If ever one is to pray—if ever one is to feel grave and anxious—if ever one is to shrink from vain show and vain babble, surely it is just on the occasion of two human beings binding themselves to one another, for better and for worse till death part them."—*Letters and Memorials of Jane Welsh Carlyle.*

An elderly unmarried lady of Scotland, after reading aloud to her two sisters, also unmarried, the births, marriages, and deaths in the ladies' corner of a newspaper, thus moralized: "Weel, weel, these are solemn events—death and marriage; but ye ken they're what we must all come to." "Eh, Miss Jeanny, but ye have been lang spared!" was the reply of the youngest sister. Those who in our thoughts were represented as being only in prospect of marriage are spared no longer. They have now come to what they had to come to—a day "so full of gladness, and so full of pain"—a day only second in importance to the day of birth; in a word, to their wedding day.

> "Are [they] sad or merry?
> Like to the time o' the year between the extremes
> Of hot and cold: [they are] nor sad nor merry."

And yet few on such a day are as collected as the late Duke of Sutherland is said to have been. Just two hours before the time fixed for his marriage with one of the most beautiful women in England, a friend came upon him in St. James's Park, leaning carelessly over the railings at the edge of the water, throwing crumbs to the waterfowl. "What! you here to-day! I thought you were going to be married this morning?" "Yes," replied the duke, without moving an inch or stopping his crumb-throwing, "I believe I am."

To men of a shyer and more nervous temperament, to be married without chloroform is a very painful operation. They find it difficult to screw their courage to the marrying place. On one occasion a bridegroom so far forgot what was due to himself and his bride as to render himself unfit to take the vows through too frequent recourse on the wedding morn to the cup that cheers—and inebriates. The minister was obliged to refuse to proceed with the marriage. A few days later, the same thing occurred with the same couple; whereupon the minister gravely remonstrated with the bride, and said they must not again present themselves with the bridegroom in such a state. "But, sir, he—*he winna come when he's sober,*" was the candid rejoinder. It is possible that this bridegroom, whose courage was so very Dutch, might have been deterred by the impending fuss and publicity of a marriage ceremony, rather than by any fear of or want of affection for her who was to become his wife. Even in the best assorted marriages there is always more or less anxiety felt upon the wedding-day.

The possibility of a hitch arising from a sudden change of inclination on the part of the principals is ludicrously illustrated by the case of two couples who on one occasion presented themselves at the Mayoralty, in a suburb of Paris, to carry out the civil portion of their marriage contract. During the ceremony one of the bridegrooms saw, or fancied he saw, his partner making "sheep's-eyes" at the bridegroom opposite. Being of a jealous temperament, he laid his hand roughly on her arm, and said sharply: "Mademoiselle, which of the two brides are you? You are mine, I believe: then oblige me by confining your glances to me." The bride was a young woman of spirit, and resenting the tone in which the reprimand was made, retorted: "Ah, Monsieur, if you are jealous already, I am likely to lead a pleasant life with you!" The jealous bridegroom made an angry reply; and then the other bridegroom must needs put his oar in. This led to a general dispute, which the Mayor in vain endeavoured to quell. The bridegrooms stormed at each other; and the brides, between their hysterical sobs, mutually accused each other of perfidy. At length the Mayor, as a last resource, adjourned the ceremony for half an hour, to admit of an amicable understanding being arrived at, both brides having refused to proceed with the celebration of the nuptials. When, at the expiration of the half-hour, the parties were summoned to reappear, they did so, to the amazement of the bewildered Mayor, in an altogether different order from that in which they had originally entered. The bridegrooms had literally effected an exchange of brides—the jealous bridegroom taking the jealous bride; and the other, the lady whose fickle glances had led to the rupture. All four adhering to the new arrangement, the Mayor, it is recorded, had no alternative but to proceed with the ceremony.

The ruling passion is not more strongly felt in death than in marriage. Dr. Johnson displayed the sturdiness of his character as he journeyed with the lady of his choice from Birmingham to Derby, at which last place they were to be married. Their ride thither, which we give in the bridegroom's own words, is an amusing bit of literary history. "Sir, she had read the old romances, and had got into her head the fantastical notion that a woman of spirit should use her lover like a dog. So, sir, at first she told me that I rode too fast, and she could not keep up with me: and when I rode a little slower, she passed me, and complained that I lagged behind. I was not to be made the slave of caprice; and I resolved to begin as I meant to end. I therefore pushed on briskly, till I was fairly out of her sight. The road lay between two hedges, so I was sure she could not miss it; and I contrived that she should soon come up with me. When she did, I observed her to be in tears."

On the wedding-day of the celebrated M. Pasteur, who has made such extraordinary discoveries about germs, the hour appointed for the ceremony had arrived, but the bridegroom was not there. Some friends rushed off to the laboratory and found him very busy with his apron on. He was excessively cross at being disturbed, and declared that marriage might wait, but his experiments could not do so.

He would indeed be a busy man who could not make time for a marriage ceremony as brief as that which was employed in the celebration of a marriage in Iowa, United States. The bride and bridegroom were told to join their hands, and then asked: "Do you want one another?" Both replied: "Yes." "Well, then, have one another;" and the couple were man and wife. Most people, however, desire a more reverent solemnization of marriage, which may be viewed in two aspects—as a natural institution, and as a religious ordinance. In the Old Testament we see it as a natural institution; in the New, it is brought before us in a religious light. It is there likened to the union of Christ and the Church. The union of Christ and the Church is not illustrated by marriage, but marriage by this spiritual union; that is, the natural is based upon the spiritual. And this is what is wanted; it gives marriage a religious signification, and it thus becomes a kind of semi-sacrament. The illustration teaches that in order to be happy though married the principle of sacrifice must rule the conduct of the married. As no love between man and wife can be true which does not issue in a sacrifice of each for the other, so Christ gave Himself for His Church and the Church sacrifices itself to His service. The only true love is self-devotion, and the every-day affairs of married life must fail without this principle of self-sacrifice or the cross of Christ.

"Would to God that His dear Son were bidden to all weddings as to that of Cana! Truly then the wine of consolation and blessing would never be lacking. He who desires that the young of his flock should be like Jacob's, fair and ring-straked, must set fair objects before their eyes; and he who would find a blessing in his marriage, must ponder the holiness and dignity of this mystery, instead of which too often weddings become a season of mere feasting and disorder."

A new home is being formed in reference to which the bride and groom should think, "This is none other but the house of God, and this is the gate of heaven. As for me and my house, we will serve the Lord." The parish church is called "God's House;" but if all the parishioners rightly used their matrimony, every house in the parish might be called the same. Home is the place of the highest joys; religion should sanctify it. Home is the sphere of the deepest sorrows; the highest consolation of religion should assuage its griefs. Home is the place of the greatest intimacy of heart with heart; religion should sweeten it with the joy of confidence. Home discovers all faults; religion should bless it with the abundance of charity. Home is the place for impressions, for instruction and culture; there should religion open her treasures of wisdom and pronounce her heavenly benediction.

An old minister previous to the meeting of the General Assembly of the Church of Scotland used to pray that the assembly might be so guided as "*no to do ony harm.*" We have often thought that such a prayer as this would be an appropriate commencement for the marriage service. Considering the issues that are involved in marriage—the misery unto the third and fourth generation that may result from it—those who join together man and woman in matrimony ought to pray that in doing so they may do no harm. Certainly the opening exhortation of the Church of England marriage service is sufficiently serious. It begins by proclaiming the sacredness of marriage as a Divine institution; hallowed as a type of the mystical union between Christ and His Church; honoured (even in its festive aspect) by Our Lord's presence and first miracle at Cana of Galilee; declared to be "honourable among all men; and therefore not by any to be enterprised, nor taken in hand, unadvisedly, lightly, or wantonly; but reverently, discreetly, advisedly, soberly, and in the fear of God; duly considering the causes for which Matrimony was ordained." These are explained in words plain-spoken almost to coarseness before allusion is made to the higher moral relation of "mutual society, help, and comfort" which marriage creates.

Then follows "the betrothal" in which the man "plights his troth" (pledges his truth), taking the initiative, while the woman gives hers in return:

"The 'wilt thou,' answered, and again
The 'wilt thou' asked, till out of twain
Her sweet 'I will' has made ye one."

The "joining of hands" is from time immemorial the pledge of covenant—we "shake hands over a bargain"—and is here an essential part of the marriage ceremony.

The use of the ring is described in the prayer that follows as the token of the marriage covenant—from the man the token of his confiding to his wife all authority over what is his, and for the woman the badge of belonging to his house. The old service has a quaint rubric declaring it put on the fourth finger of the left hand, because thence "there is a vein leading direct to the heart." The Prayer Book of Edward VI. directs that "the man shall give unto the woman a ring, and other tokens of spousage, as gold or silver, laying the same upon the book." This is clearly the ancient bride price. Wheatly's "Book of Common Prayer" says, "This lets us into the design of the ring, and intimates it to be the remains of an ancient custom whereby it was usual for the man to purchase the woman." The words to be spoken by the man are taken from the old service, still using the ancient word "worship" (worth—ship) for service and honour. They declare the dedication both of person and substance to the marriage bond.

The Blessing is one of singular beauty and solemnity. It not only invokes God's favour to "bless, preserve, and keep" the newly-made husband and wife in this world, but looks beyond it to the life hereafter, for which nothing can so well prepare them as a well-spent wedded life here.

It is said that among the natives of India the cost to a father of marrying his daughter is about equal to having his house burnt down. Although brides are not so expensive in this country much money is wasted on the wedding and preliminaries which would be very useful to the young people a year or two afterwards.

We would not advise that there should be no wedding-breakfast and that the bride should have no trousseau; but we do think that these accessories should be in accordance with the family exchequer. Again, wedding presents are often the very articles that the young couple need least, and are not unfrequently found to be duplicates of the gifts of other persons. But we cannot linger over the wedding festivities.

Adieu, young friends! and may joy crown you, love bless you, God speed your career!

"Some natural tears they dropp'd, but wip'd them soon;
The world was all before them, where to choose
Their place of rest, and Providence their guide.
They, hand in hand, with wand'ring steps and slow,
Through Eden took their solitary way."

CHAPTER IX.

HONEYMOONING.

"The importance of the honeymoon, which had been so much vaunted to him by his father, had not held good."—*The Married Life of Albert Durer.*

The "honeymoon" is defined by Johnson to be "the first month after marriage, when there is nothing but tenderness and pleasure." And certainly it ought to be the happiest month in our lives; but it may, like every other good thing, be spoiled by mismanagement. When this is the case, we take our honeymoon like other pleasures—sadly. Instead of happy reminiscences, nothing is left of it except its jars.

You take, says the philosophical observer, a man and a woman, who in nine cases out of ten know very little about each other (though they generally fancy they do), you cut off the woman from all her female friends, you deprive the man of his ordinary business and ordinary pleasures, and you condemn this unhappy pair to spend a month of enforced seclusion in each other's society. If they marry in the summer and start on a tour, the man is oppressed with a plethora of sight-seeing, while the lady, as often as not, becomes seriously ill from fatigue and excitement.

A newly-married man took his bride on a tour to Switzerland for the honeymoon, and when there induced her to attempt with him the ascent of one of the high peaks. The lady, who at home had never ascended a hill higher than a church, was much alarmed, and had to be carried by the guides with her eyes blindfolded, so as not to witness the horrors of the passage. The bridegroom walked close to her, expostulating respecting her fear. He spoke in honeymoon whispers; but the rarefaction of the air was such that every word was audible. "You told me, Leonora, that you always felt happy—no matter where you were—so long as you were in my company. Then why are you not happy now?" "Yes, Charles, I did," replied she; sobbing hysterically; "but I never meant above the snow line." It is at such times as these that awkward angles of temper make themselves manifest, which, under a more sensible system, might have been concealed for years, perhaps for ever.

Boswell called upon Dr. Johnson on the morning of the day on which he was to leave for Scotland—for matrimonial purposes. The prospect of connubial felicity had made the expectant husband voluble; he therefore took courage to recite to the sage a little love-song which he had himself composed and which Dibdin was to set to music:

A Matrimonial Thought.

"In the blythe days of honeymoon,
With Kate's allurements smitten,
I loved her late, I loved her soon,
And called her dearest kitten.

But now my kitten's grown a cat,
And cross like other wives,
Oh! by my soul, my honest Mat,
I fear she has nine lives."

Johnson: "It is very well, sir, but you should not swear." Whereupon the obnoxious "Oh! by my soul," was changed on the instant to "Alas! alas!"

If the kitten should develop into a cat even before the "blythe days of honeymoon" are ended, it is no wonder, considering the way some young couples spend the first month of married life, rushing from one continental city to another, and visiting all the churches and picture-galleries, however scorching may be the weather or however great may be their secret aversion to art and antiquity. The lady gives way to fatigue, and is seized with a violent headache. For a while the young husband thinks that it is rather nice to support his Kate's head, but when she answers his sympathetic inquiries sharply and petulantly, he in turn becomes less amiable, dazzling, enchanting, and, in a word, all that as a *fiancé* he had been.

Winter honeymooning is even more trying to the temper, for then short days and unfavourable weather compel the young couple to stay in one place. Imagine the delights of a month spent in lodgings at the seaside, with nothing to do except to get photographed, which is a favourite pastime of the newly-married. The bride may be indifferent to the rain and sleet beating against the windows, for she can spend the time writing to her friends long and enthusiastic descriptions of her happiness; but what can the unlucky bridegroom do? He subscribes to the circulating library, reads a series of novels aloud to his wife, and illustrates every amatory passage with a kiss. But the "dear old boy" (as the bride calls him) tires of this sort of thing after a week, and how can he then amuse himself? He stares out of windows, he watches the arrival of the milkman and the butcher with the liveliest interest; he envies the coastguardsman, who is perpetually on the look-out for invisible smugglers through a portentously long telescope. Cases have been known where the bridegroom—a City man—being driven to desperation, has privately ordered the office journal and ledger to be sent down by luggage train, and has devoted his evenings to checking the additions in those interesting volumes.

When Hodge and his sweetheart crown their pastoral loves in the quiet old country church, they take a pleasant drive or a walk in their finery, and settle down at once to connubial comfort in the cot beside the wood. Why do their richer neighbours deny themselves this happiness and invent special troubles? Why, during the early weeks of married life, do they lay up sad memories of provoking mistakes, of trunks which will not pack, of trains which will not wait, of tiresome sight-seeing, of broiling sun, of headache, of "the fretful stir unprofitable, and the fever" of honeymooning abroad? Many a bridegroom but just returned from a "delightful tour on the Continent" will be able to sympathize in the remark of the country farmer to a companion in the train, as he went to town to buy hay. "Yes, it's been a bad winter for some folk. Old Smith's dead, and so is Jones, and my wife died yesterday. And how be the hay, master?"

We do not want excitement during the honeymoon, for are we not in love (if we are not we ought to be ashamed of ourselves), and is not love all-sufficient? Last week we only saw the object of our affections by fits and starts as it were; now we have her or him all to ourselves.

"Who hath not felt that breath in the air,
A perfume and freshness strange and rare,
A warmth in the light, and a bliss everywhere,
When young hearts yearn together?
All sweets below, and all sunny above,
Oh! there's nothing in life like making love,
Save making hay in fine weather."

Let cynics say what they will, the honeymoon, when not greatly mismanaged, *is* a halcyon period. It is a delightful lull between two distinct states of existence, and the married man is not to be envied who can recall no pleasant reminiscences of it. What profane outsiders consider very dull has a charm of its own to honeymoon lovers who "illumine life with dreaming," and who see—

"Golden visions wave and hover,
Golden vapours, waters streaming,
Landscapes moving, changing, gleaming!"

Still, we cannot but think that if a wedding tour must be taken it should be short, quiet, free-and-easy, and inexpensive. At some future time, when the young people are less agitated and have learned to understand each other better, the time and money saved will be available for a more extended holiday. During the honeymoon there should be "marches hymeneal in the land of the ideal" rather than globe-trotting; "thoughts moved o'er fields Elysian" rather than over the perplexing pages of "Bradshaw's General Railway and Steam Navigation Guide."

In reference to the honeymoon, as to other matters, people's opinions differ according to their temperaments and circumstances. So we shall conclude this chapter by quoting two nearly opposite opinions, and ask our readers to decide for themselves.

In the "Memoir of Daniel Macmillan" his opinion is thus stated: "That going out for the honeymoon is a most wise and useful invention; it enables you to be so constantly together, and to obtain a deeper knowledge of each other; and it also helps one to see and feel the preciousness of such intimacy as nothing else could. Intercourse in the presence of others never leads below the surface, and it is in the very depths of our being that true calm, deep and true peace and love lie. Nothing so well prepares for the serious duties of after-life."

"As to long honeymoons," says the Bishop of Rochester, "most sensible people have come utterly to disbelieve in them. They are a forced homage to utterly false ideas; they are a waste of money at a moment when every shilling is wanted for much more pressing objects; they are a loss of time, which soon comes to be dreary and weary. Most of all, they are a risk for love, which ought not so soon to be so unpleasantly tested by the inevitable petulances of a secret *ennui*. Six days by all means, and then, oh! happy friends, go straight home.... Whenever you come back, six weeks hence or one, you will have just as much to stand the fire of a little hard staring which won't hurt you, and of bright pleasantness which need not vex you; and the sooner you are at home, the sooner you will find out what married happiness means."

CHAPTER X.

MARRIAGE VOWS.

"Better is it that thou shouldest not vow, than that thou shouldest vow and not pay."—*Ecclesiastes* v. 5.

The honeymoon is over, and our young couple have exchanged their chrysalis condition for the pleasures and duties of ordinary married life. Let them begin by forming the highest ideal of marriage. Now, and on every anniversary of their wedding day, they should seriously reflect upon those vows which are too often taken, either in entire ignorance of their meaning and import, or thoughtlessly, as though they were mere incidents of the marriage ceremony.

A Hampshire incumbent recently reported some of the blunders he had heard made in the marriage service, by that class of persons who have to pick up the words as best they can from hearing them repeated by others. He said that in his own parish it was quite the fashion for the man, when giving the ring, to say to the woman: "With my body I thee wash up, and with all my hurdle goods I thee and thou." He said the women were generally better up in this part of the service than the men. One day, however, a bride startled him by promising, in what she supposed to be language of the Prayer Book, to take her husband "to 'ave and to 'old from this day fortn't, for betterer horse, for richerer power, in siggerness health, to love cherries, and to bay." We have heard of an ignorant bridegroom, who, confusing the baptismal and marriage services, replied, when asked if he consented to take the bride for his wife: "I renounce them all!" It is to be hoped that the times of such ignorance are either passed or passing; still, a little instruction in reference to marriage vows might be given with advantage in some churches.

In one of his letters Byron tells a story of a learned Jew, who was remarkable, in the brilliant circles to which his learning gained him admittance, for his habit of asking questions continuously and fearlessly, in order to get at the bottom of any matter in discussion. To a person who was complaining of the Prince Regent's bad treatment of his old boon companions, this habitual interrogator cried across a dinner-table: "And why does the prince act so?" "Because he was told so-and-so by Lord ——; who ought to be ashamed of himself!" was the answer. "But why, sir, has the prince cut *you*?" inquired the searcher after truth. "Because I stuck to my principles—yes, sir, because I stuck to my principles!" replied the other, testily, thinking that his examination was ended. "*And why did you stick to your principles?*" cried the interrogator, throwing the table into a roar of laughter, the mirth being no more due to the inquisitor's persistence than to his inability to conceive that any man would stick to his principles simply because he believed them to be right. Are there not some educated as well as uneducated people who seem to be quite as incapable of conceiving that they should keep their marriage vows, simply because it is dishonourable and wicked to break them?

A mother having become alarmed about the failing state of her daughter's health, and not being able to get much satisfaction from a consultation with the village doctor, took her to a London physician for further advice. He asked a few questions as to the girl's daily habits and mode of life, carefully stethoscoped her heart and lungs, and then gave an involuntary sigh. The mother grew pale, and waited anxiously for a verdict "Madam," he said, "so far as I can discover, your daughter is suffering from a most serious complaint, which, for want of a better name, I shall call 'dulness.' Perhaps it is in your power to cure it. I have no medicine which is a specific for this disease." Girls, who suffer in this way, too often prescribe for themselves marriage with men whom they cannot love, honour, and obey. This is as bad as dram-drinking, or gambling; but what else can the poor things do? They have not been trained like their brothers to useful work, and have always been told that woman's first, best occupation is—to be a wife. To which it may be answered—

"Most true; but to make a mere business of marriage,
To call it a 'living,' 'vocation,' 'career,'
Is but to pervert, to degrade, and disparage
A contract of all the most sacred and dear."

Nor will those vows be regarded with greater sanctity which are taken against the inclination. Better to be as candid as the girl who, forced by her parents into a disagreeable match, when the clergyman came to that part of the service where the bride is asked if she will have the bridegroom for her husband, said, with great simplicity, "Oh dear, no, sir; but you are the first person who has asked my opinion about the matter!"

Let us think now what the vows are which, at the altar of God, and in the presence of our fellow-creatures, we solemnly vow. Both the man and the woman vow to love, honour, cherish, and be faithful, for better for worse, for richer for poorer, in sickness and health, till death part them. Then the husband promises to comfort his wife, and the wife to serve and obey her husband.

A Scotch lady, whose daughter was recently married, was asked by an old friend whether she might congratulate her upon the event. "Yes, yes," she answered; "upon the whole it is very satisfactory; it is true Jeannie hates her gudeman, but then there's always a something." The old friend might have told this Scotch lady that in making light of love she made light of that which was needful to hallow her daughter's marriage; and that even the blessing of a bishop in the most fashionable church does not prevent a loveless alliance from being a sacrifice of true chastity.

Contrast the indifference of this Scotch lady in reference to matrimonial love, with the value set upon it in a letter which Pliny the Younger, who was a heathen, wrote concerning his wife, Calpurnia, to her aunt. It is quoted by Dr. Cook as follows: "She loves me, the surest pledge of her virtue, and adds to this a wonderful disposition to learning, which she has acquired from her affection to me. She reads my writings, studies them, and even gets them by heart. You would smile to see the concern she is in when I have a cause to plead, and the joy she shows when it is over. She finds means to have the first news brought her of the success I meet with in court. If I recite anything in public, she cannot refrain from placing herself privately in some corner to hear. Sometimes she accompanies my verses with the lute, without any master except love—the best of instructors. From these instances I take the most certain omens of our perpetual and increasing happiness, since her affection is not founded on my youth or person, which must gradually decay; but she is in love with the immortal part of me."

The second vow taken by both the man and the woman is to "honour." "Likewise, ye husbands, dwell with them according to knowledge, giving honour unto the wife as unto the weaker vessel." "And the wife see that she reverence her husband." The weaker vessel is to be honoured, not because she is weak, but because, being weak, she acts her part so well.

And even if the wife's courage and endurance should sometimes fail, a good husband would not withhold honour from her on that account. He would remember her weaker nature, and her more delicate physical frame, her more acute nervous sensibility, her greater sensitiveness and greater trials, the peculiar troubles to which she is subject.

In a lately published "Narrative of a Journey through the South China Border Lands," we are told that a wife in this part of the world, when mentioned by her husband, "which happens as seldom as possible," is called "My dull thorn," "The thorn in my ribs," or "The mean one of the inner rooms." This is the way *not* to honour a wife. But the honour which a husband should give is not merely that chivalrous bearing which the strong owe to the weak, and which every woman has a right to expect from every man. In describing a husband who was in the habit of honouring his wife, Dr. Landels remarks that "one could not be in his presence without feeling it. Never a word escaped his lips which reflected directly or indirectly on her. Never an action he performed would have led to the impression that there could be any difference between them. She was the queen of his home. All about them felt that in his estimation, and by his desire, her authority was unimpeachable, and her will law. And the effect of his example was that children and friends and domestics alike hedged her about with sweet respect. A man of strong will himself, his was never known to be in collision with hers; and, without any undue yielding, the homage which he paid to his wife made their union one of the happiest it has ever been our privilege to witness."

And the wife, on her part, is to reverence and honour her husband as long as she possibly can. If possible, she should let her husband suppose that she thinks him a *good* husband, and it will be a strong stimulus to his being so. As long as he thinks he possesses the character, he will take some pains to deserve it; but when he has lost the name he will be very apt to abandon the reality altogether. "To treat men as if they were better than they are is the surest way to *make* them better than they are." Keats tells us that he has met with women who would like to be married to a Poem, and given away by a Novel; but wives must not cease to honour their husbands on discovering that instead of being poetical and romantic they are very ordinary, imperfect beings.

There are homes where poverty has never left its pinch nor sickness paid its visit; homes where there is plenty on the board, and health in the circle, and yet where a skeleton more grim than death haunts the cupboard, and an ache harsher than consumption's tooth gnaws sharply at the heart. Why do those shoulders stoop so early ere life's noon has passed? Why is it that the sigh which follows the closing of the door after the husband has gone off to business is a sigh of relief, and that which greets his coming footstep is a sigh of dread? What means that nervous pressing of the hand against the heart, the gulping back of the lump that rises in the throat, the forced smile, and the pressed-back tear? If we could but speak to the husbands who haunt these homes, we would tell them that some such soliloquy as the following is ever passing like a laboured breath through the distracted minds of their wives: "Is this the Canaan, this the land of promise, this the milk and honey that were pictured to my fancy; when the walks among the lanes, and fields, and flowers were all too short, and the whispers were so loving, and the pressure was so fond, and the heart-beat was so passionate? For what have I surrendered home, youth, beauty, freedom, love—all that a woman has to give in all her wealth of confidence? Harsh tones, cold looks, stern words, short answers, sullen reserve." "What," says the cheery neighbour, "is that all?" All! What more is needed to make home dark, to poison hope, to turn life into a funeral, the marriage-robe into a shroud, and the grave into a refuge? It does not want drunkenness, blows, bruises, clenched fists, oaths, to work sacrilege in the temple of the home; only a little ice where the fire should glow; only a cold look where the love should burn; only a sneer where there ought to be a smile. Husband! that wife of yours is wretched because you are a liar; because you perjured yourself when you vowed to love and cherish. You are too great a coward to beat her brains out with a poker lest the gallows claim you; but you are so little of a man that you poison her soul with the slow cruelty of an oath daily foresworn and brutally ignored. If the ducking-stool was a punishment of old for a scolding wife, a fiercer baptism should await the husband who has ceased to cherish his wife.

As regards the vow of fidelity we need only quote these words of the prophet Malachi: "The Lord hath been witness between thee and the wife of thy youth, against whom thou hast dealt treacherously: yet she is thy companion, and the wife of thy covenant. And did not he make one? Therefore take heed to your spirit, and let none deal treacherously against the wife of his youth." But there are absentee husbands and wives who, though they are not guilty of breaking the seventh commandment, do by no means keep the promise of keeping only to their wives and husbands. If a man come home only when other places are shut, or when his money is all gone, or when nobody else wants him, is he not telling his wife and family, as plainly by deeds as he could possibly by words, that he takes more delight in other company than in theirs? Charles Lamb used to feel that there was something of dishonesty in any pleasures which he took without his lunatic sister. A good man will feel something like this in reference to his wife and children.

But though men should love their homes, it is quite possible for them to be too much at home. This at least is the opinion of most wives. There is everywhere a disposition to pack off the men in the morning and to bid them keep out of the way till towards evening, when it is assumed they will probably have a little news of the busy world to bring home, and when baby will be sure to have said something exceptionally brilliant and precocious. The general events of the day will afford topics of conversation more interesting by far than if the whole household had been together from morning till night. Men about home all day are fidgety, grumpy, and interfering—altogether objectionable, in short.

As a rule it is when things are going wrong that women show to the best advantage. Every one can remember illustrations. We have one in the following story of Hawthorne, which was told to Mr. Conway by an intimate friend of the novelist. One wintry day Hawthorne received at his office notification that his services would no longer be required. With heaviness of heart he repaired to his humble home. His young wife recognizes the change and stands waiting for the silence to be broken. At length he falters, "I am removed from office." Then she leaves the room; she returns with fuel and kindles a bright fire with her own hands; next she brings pen, paper, ink, and sets them beside him. Then she touches the sad man on the shoulder, and, as he turns to the beaming face, says, "Now you can write your book." The cloud cleared away. The lost office looked like a cage from which he had escaped. "The Scarlet Letter" was written, and a marvellous success rewarded the author and his stout-hearted wife.

The care some wives take of their husbands in sickness is very touching. John Richard Green, the historian, whose death seemed so untimely, is an instance of this. His very life was prolonged in the most wonderful way by the care and skill with which he was tended; and it was with and through his wife that the work was done which he could not have done alone. She consulted the authorities for him, examined into obscure points, and wrote to his dictation. In this way, when he could not work more than two hours in the day, and when often some slight change in the weather would throw him back and make work impossible for days or weeks, the book was prepared which he published under the title of "The Making of England."

The husband's vow to "comfort" was never better performed than by Cobbett. In his "Advice to Young Men" he says: "I began my young marriage days in and near Philadelphia. At one of those times to which I have just alluded, in the middle of the burning hot month of July, I was greatly afraid of fatal consequences to my wife for want of sleep, she not having, after the great danger was over, had any sleep for more than forty-eight hours. All great cities in hot countries are, I believe, full of dogs, and they, in the very hot weather, keep up during the night a horrible barking and fighting and howling. Upon the particular occasion to which I am adverting they made a noise so terrible and so unremitted that it was next to impossible that even a person in full health and free from pain should obtain a minute's sleep. I was, about nine in the evening, sitting by the bed. 'I do think,' said she, 'that I could go to sleep *now*, if it were not *for the dogs*.' Downstairs I went, and out I sallied, in my shirt and trousers, and without shoes and stockings; and, going to a heap of stones lying beside the road, set to work upon the dogs, going backward and forward, and keeping them at two or three hundred yards' distance from the house. I walked thus the whole night, barefooted, lest the noise of my shoes might possibly reach her ears; and I remember that the bricks of the causeway were, even in the night, so hot as to be disagreeable to my feet. My exertions produced the desired effect: a sleep of several hours was the consequence, and, at eight o'clock in the morning, off went I to a day's business which was to end at six in the evening.

"Women are all patriots of the soil; and when her neighbours used to ask my wife whether *all* English husbands were like hers, she boldly answered in the affirmative. I had business to occupy the whole of my time, Sundays and week-days, except sleeping hours; but I used to make time to assist her in the taking care of her baby, and in all sorts of things: get up, light her fire, boil her tea-kettle, carry her up warm water in cold weather, take the child while she dressed herself and got the breakfast ready, then breakfast, get her in water and wood for the day, then dress myself neatly and sally forth to my business. The moment that was over I used to hasten back to her again; and I no more thought of spending a moment *away from her*, unless business compelled me, than I thought of quitting the country and going to sea. The *thunder* and *lightning* are tremendous in America compared with what they are in England. My wife was at one time very much afraid of thunder and lightning; and, as is the feeling of all such women, and indeed all men too, she wanted company, and particularly her husband, in those times of danger. I knew well of course that my presence would not diminish the danger; but, be I at what I might, if within reach of home, I used to quit my business and hasten to her the moment I perceived a thunderstorm approaching. Scores of miles have I, first and last, *run* on this errand in the streets of Philadelphia! The Frenchmen who were my scholars used to laugh at me exceedingly on this account; and sometimes, when I was making an appointment with them, they would say, with a smile and a bow, '*Sauve le tonnerre toujours, Monsieur Cobbett!*'"

Much is said both wise and otherwise in reference to the obedience which a wife vows to yield to her husband. One who wrote a sketch of the Rev. F. D. Maurice tells us that he met him once at a wedding breakfast. Maurice proposed the health of the bride and bridegroom. The lady turned round, and in rather bad taste exclaimed, "Now, Mr. Maurice, I call you to witness that I entertain no intention of obeying." Maurice answered with his sad, sweet smile, "Ah, madam, you little know the blessedness of obedience."

Of course no one believes that it is a wife's duty to obey when her husband wishes her to act contrary to the dictates of conscience. As little is she expected to conform to a standard of obedience and service such as was laid down in a conversation overheard between two children who were playing on the sands together. Small boy to little girl: "Do you wish to be my wife?" Little girl, after reflection; "Yes." Small boy: "Then pull off my boots." We all rejoice in the fact that woman's rights are very different now from what they used to be, at least in Russia, where, Dr. Lansdell tells us, anciently at a wedding the bridegroom took to church a whip, and in one part of the ceremony lightly applied it to the bride's back, in token that she was to be in subjection. Is there not still, however, much truth in the old couplet:

"Man, love thy wife; thy husband, wife, obey.
Wives are our heart; we should be head alway"?

On a great many points concerning the pecuniary or other interests of the family, the husband will usually be the wisest, and may most properly be treated as the senior or acting partner in the firm.

"The good wife," says Fuller, "commandeth her husband in any equal matter, by constantly obeying him. It was always observed, that what the English gained of the French in battle by valour, the French regained of the English in cunning by treaties. So if the husband should chance by his power in his passion to prejudice his wife's right, she wisely knoweth by compounding and complying, to recover and rectify it again." This is very much what the well-known lines in "Hiawatha" teach—

"As unto the bow the cord is,
So unto the man is woman;
Though she bends him, she obeys him;
Though she draws him, yet she follows;
Useless each without the other!"

But indeed it is a sign of something being wrong between married people, when the question which of the two shall be subject to the other ever arises. It will never do so when both parties love as they ought, for then the struggle will be not who shall command and control, but who shall serve and yield. As Chaucer says—

"When mastery cometh, then sweet Love anon,
Flappeth his nimble wings and soon away is flown."

CHAPTER XI.

"DRIVE GENTLY OVER THE STONES!"

"It were better to meet some dangers half-way, though they come nothing near."—*Bacon.*

"Rocks whereon greatest men have oftest wreck'd."—*Milton.*

"Drive gently over the stones!" This piece of advice, which is frequently given to inexperienced whips, may be suggested metaphorically to the newly-married. On the road upon which they have entered there are stony places, which, if not carefully driven over, will almost certainly upset the domestic coach. To accompany one's wife harmoniously on an Irish car is easy compared to the task of accompanying her over these stones on the domestic car.

The first rock ahead which should be signalled "dangerous" is the first year of married life. As a rule the first year either mars or makes a marriage. During this period errors may be committed which will cast a shadow over every year that follows. We agree with Mrs. Jameson in thinking that the first year of married life is not as happy as the second. People have to get into the habit of being married, and there are difficult lessons to be learned in the apprenticeship.

A lady once asked Dr. Johnson how in his dictionary he came to define *pastern* the *knee* of a horse; he immediately answered, "Ignorance, madam, pure ignorance." This is the simple explanation of many an accident that takes place at the commencement of the matrimonial journey. The young couple have not yet learned the dangerous places of the road, and, as a consequence, they drive carelessly over them.

How many people starting in married life throw happiness out of their grasp, and create troubles for the rest of their days! The cause may be generally traced to selfishness, their conceit taking everything that goes amiss as meant for a personal affront, and their wounded self-esteem making life a burden hard to bear, for themselves and others. We can all recognize in every circle such cases; we are all able to read the moral elsewhere; but in our own case we allow the small breach—that might be healed with very little effort at first—to get wider and wider, and the pair that should become closer and closer, gradually not only cease to care for, but have a dread of each other's society.

There is one simple direction, which, if carefully regarded, might long preserve the tranquillity of the married life, and ensure no inconsiderable portion of connubial happiness to the observers of it: it is—to beware of the *first* dispute. "Man and wife," says Jeremy Taylor, "are equally concerned to avoid all offences of each other in the beginning of their conversation; every little thing can blast an infant blossom; and the breath of the south can shake the little rings of the vine, when first they begin to curl like the locks of a new weaned boy: but when by age and consolidation they stiffen into the hardness of a stem, and have, by the warm embraces of the sun and the kisses of heaven, brought forth their clusters, they can endure the storms of the north, and the loud noises of a tempest, and yet never be broken. So are the early unions of an unfixed marriage; watchful and observant, jealous and busy, inquisitive and careful, and apt to take alarm at every unkind word. After the hearts of the man and the wife are endeared and hardened by a mutual confidence and experience, longer than artifice and pretence can last, there are a great many remembrances, and some things present, that dash all little unkindnesses in pieces."

Every little dispute between man and wife is dangerous. It forces good-humour out of its channel, undermines affection, and insidiously, though perhaps insensibly, wears out and, at last, entirely destroys that cordiality which is the life and soul of matrimonial felicity. As however "it's hardly in a body's power to keep at times from being sour," undue importance ought not to be attached to "those little tiffs that sometimes cast a shade on wedlock." Often they are, as the poet goes on to observe, "love in masquerade—

"And family jars, look we but o'er the rim,
Are filled with honey, even to the brim."

In the Life of St. Francis de Sales we are told that the saint did not approve of the saying, "Never rely on a reconciled enemy." He rather preferred a contrary maxim, and said that a quarrel between friends, when made up, added a new tie to friendship; as experience shows that the calosity formed round a broken bone makes it stronger than before.

Beware of jealousy; "it is the green-eyed monster, which doth make the meat it feeds on." Here is an amusing case in point. A French lady who was jealous of her husband determined to watch his movements. One day, when he told her he was going to Versailles, she followed him, keeping him in sight until she missed him in a passage leading to the railway station. Looking about her for a few minutes, she saw a man coming out of a glove-shop with a rather overdressed lady. Blinded with rage and jealousy, she fancied it was her husband, and without pausing for a moment to consider, bounced suddenly up to him and gave him three or four stinging boxes on the ear. The instant the gentleman turned round, she discovered her mistake, and at the same moment caught sight of her husband, who had merely called at a tobacconist's, and was now crossing the street. There was nothing for it but to faint in the arms of the gentleman she had attacked; while the other lady moved away, to avoid a scene. The stranger, astonished to find an unknown lady in his arms, was further startled by a gentleman seizing him by the collar and demanding to know what he meant by embracing that lady. "Why, sir, she boxed my ears, and then fainted," exclaimed the innocent victim. "She is my wife," shouted the angry husband, "and would never have struck you without good cause." Worse than angry words would probably have followed had not the cause of the whole misunderstanding recovered sufficiently to explain how it had all happened.

A jealous wife is generally considered a proper subject for ridicule; and a woman ought to conceal from her husband any feeling of the kind. Her suspicions may be altogether groundless, and she may be tormenting herself with a whole train of imaginary evils.

On the other hand a husband is bound to abstain from even the appearance of preferring any one else to his wife. When in the presence of others he should indulge her laudable pride by showing that he thinks her an object of importance and preference.

In his "Advice to Young Men" Cobbett gives this interesting bit of autobiography. "For about two or three years after I was married, I, retaining some of my military manners, used, both in France and America, to *romp* most famously with the girls that came in my way; till one day at Philadelphia, my wife said to me in a very gentle manner: 'Don't do that, *I do not like it*.' That was quite enough; I had never *thought* on the subject before; one hair of her head was more dear to me than all the other women in the world, and this I knew that she knew. But I now saw that this was not all that she had a right to from me; I saw that she had the further claim upon me that I should abstain from everything that might induce others to believe that there was any other woman for whom, even if I were at liberty, I had any affection. I beseech young married men to bear this in mind; for on some trifle of this sort the happiness or misery of a long life frequently turns."

There may be a fanaticism in love as well as in belief, and where people love much they are apt to be exacting one to the other. But although jealousy does imply love, such love as consists in a craving for the affection of its object, it is love which is largely dashed with selfishness. It is incompatible with love of the highest order, for where that exists there is no dread of not being loved enough in return. In this relation as well as in the highest, "There is no fear in love, but perfect love casteth out fear, because fear hath torment. He that feareth is not made perfect in love."

It is generally admitted that conjugal affection largely depends on mutual confidence. A friend quoted this sentiment the other day in a smoking-room, and added that he made it a rule to tell his wife everything that happened, and in this way they avoided any misunderstanding. "Well, sir," remarked another gentleman present, not to be outdone in generosity, "you are not so open and frank as I am, for I tell my wife a good many things that never happen." "Oh!" exclaimed a third, "I am under no necessity to keep my wife informed regarding my affairs. She can find out five times as much as I know myself without the least trouble."

"How," said a gentleman to a friend who wished to convey a matter of importance to a lady without communicating directly with her, "how can you be certain of her reading the letter, seeing that you have directed it to her husband?" "That I have managed without the possibility of failure," was the answer; "she will open it to a certainty, for I have put the word 'private' in the corner."

These anecdotes put in a lively way the well-known fact that it is impossible for married people to keep secrets the one from the other. But even to make the attempt is to enter upon ground so dangerous that scarcely any amount of cautious driving will prevent a catastrophe. Unless husband and wife trust each other all in all the result will be much the same as if they trusted not at all.

We believe that the Delilahs are few who would sell their Samsons to the Philistines when these Samsons have told them the secret source of their great strength. Still, there are secrets entrusted to the clergyman, the physician, the lawyer, the legislator to betray which, even to a wife, would be dishonourable and disgraceful.

A case beautifully illustrating this difficult point in matrimonial relations occurs in the memoirs of Lady Fanshawe, wife of Sir Richard Fanshawe, who was a faithful Royalist during the civil war. Soon after Lady Fanshawe's marriage, she was instigated by some crafty ladies of the court to obtain from her husband a knowledge of some secret political events. The matter is best described in her own words: "And now I thought myself a perfect queen, and my husband so glorious a crown, that I more valued myself to be called by his name than born a princess, for I knew him very wise and very good, and his soul doted on me; upon which confidence I will tell you what happened. My Lady Rivers, a brave woman, and one that had suffered many thousand pounds' loss for the King, and whom I had a great reverence for, and she a kindness for me as a kinswoman—in discourse she tacitly commended the knowledge of State affairs, and that some women were very happy in a good understanding thereof, as my Lady Aubingny, Lady Isabel Thynne, and divers others, and yet none was at first more capable than I; that in the night she knew there came a post from Paris from the Queen, and that she would be extremely glad to hear what the Queen commanded the King in order to his affairs; saying, if I would ask my husband privately, he would tell me what he found in the packet, and I might tell her. I that was young and innocent, and to that day had never in my mouth, what news?—began to think there was more in inquiring into public affairs than I thought of, and that it being a fashionable thing, would make me more beloved of my husband, if that had been possible, than I was. When my husband returned home from council, after welcoming him, as his custom ever was, he went with his handful of papers into his study for an hour or more; I followed him: he turned hastily and said, 'What would'st thou have, my life?' I told him, 'I heard the Prince had received a packet from the Queen, and I guessed it was that in his hands, and I desired to know what was in it.' He smilingly replied, 'My love, I will immediately come to thee; pray thee go, for I am very busy.' When he came out of his closet I revived my suit; he kissed me and talked of other things. At supper, I would eat nothing; he as usual sat by me, and drank often to me, which was his custom, and was full of discourse to company that was at table. Going to bed I asked again, and said I could not believe he loved me, if he refused to tell me all he knew; but he answered nothing, but stopped my mouth with kisses. So we went to bed; I cried, and he went to sleep. Next morning early, as his custom was, he was called to rise, but began to discourse with me first; to which I made no reply; he rose, came on the other side of the bed and kissed me, and drew the curtain softly and went to court. When he came home to dinner, he presently came to me as was usual, and when I had him by the hand, I said, 'Thou dost not care to see me troubled;' to which he, taking me in his arms, answered, 'My dearest soul, nothing upon earth can afflict me like that; and when you asked me of my business, it was wholly out of my power to satisfy thee, for my life and fortune shall be thine, and every thought of my heart in which the trust I am in may not be revealed; but my honour is my own, which I cannot preserve if I communicate the Prince's affairs; and pray thee with this answer rest satisfied.' So great was his reason and goodness, that upon consideration it made my folly appear to me so vile, that from that day until the day of his death, I never thought fit to ask him any business but what he communicated freely to me, in order to his estate and family."

When a man comes home tired, hungry, and put out about something that has gone wrong in business, this is not the time for his wife to order him to stand and deliver his secret troubles. Rather, she should give him a well-cooked dinner and say little or nothing. Later on in the evening, when he is rested and has smoked a pipe of peace, he will be only too glad to give her his confidence in return for her sympathetic treatment of him. It seems to me that there is more of vulgar familiarity than of confidence in a man and wife at all times opening each other's letters. A sealed letter is sacred; and all persons like to have the first reading of their own letters. Why should a close relationship abrogate respectful courtesy?

Artemus Ward tells us that when he was at Salt Lake he was introduced to Brigham Young's mother-in-law. "I can't exactly tell you how many there is of her, but it's a good deal." Married people require to drive gently when there is in the way the stumbling-block of "a good deal" of mother-or other relations-in-law. Certainly Adam and Eve were in paradise in this respect. "When I want a nice snug day all to myself," says an ingenuous wife, "I tell George dear mother is coming, and then I see nothing of him till one in the morning." "Are your domestic relations agreeable?" was the question put to an unhappy-looking specimen of humanity. "Oh, my domestic relations are all right; it is my wife's relations that are causing the trouble." It is true we read in the *Graphic* a year or two ago an exception to the usual dislike to mothers-in-law, but the exception was scarcely reassuring. A well-dressed young woman of nineteen informed a magistrate that her own mother had run away with her husband. This *mater pulchrior* came to stay with her *filia pulchra*, won the affections of the husband, and, at last, withdrew him from his hearth and home. Still it is the duty of people to keep on terms of at least friendly neutrality with their relations-in-law. Where there is disunion there are generally faults on both sides.

We know of a working-man who on the eve of his marriage signed a promise to abstain from intoxicating liquor. He put the document into a frame and presented it to his wife after the wedding as a marriage settlement. And certainly there cannot be a better marriage settlement than for a young husband to settle his habits.

The young husband or wife who is in the least degree careless in the use of intoxicating drinks should read the following account which Mr. Gough gives of a case which he met in one of the convict prisons of America. "I was attracted, while speaking to the prisoners in the chapel, by the patient, gentle look of one of the convicts who sat before me, whose whole appearance was that of a mild-tempered, quiet man. After the service, one of the prison officers, in reply to my question, stated that this same man was serving out a life term. I asked what was the possible crime for which he was serving a life term in a State prison. 'Murder.' 'Murder?' 'Yes, he murdered his wife.' Having asked if I might have an interview with him, my request was granted, and I held a conversation with him. 'My friend, I do not wish to ask you any questions that will be annoying; but I was struck by your appearance, and was so much surprised when I heard of your crime, that I thought I would like to ask you a question. May I?' 'Certainly, sir.' 'Then why did you commit the crime? What led you to it?' Then came such a pitiful story. He said: 'I loved my wife, but I drank to excess. She was a good woman; she never complained; come home when or how I might, she never scolded. I think I never heard a sharp word from her. She would sometimes look at me with such a pitying look that went to my heart; sometimes it made me tender, and I would cry, and promise to do better; at other times it would make me angry. I almost wished she would scold me, rather than look at me with that patient earnestness. I knew I was breaking her heart; but I was a slave to drink. Though I loved her, I knew I was killing her. One day I came home drunk, and as I entered the room I saw her sitting at the table, her face resting on her hand. Oh, my God! I think I see her now! As I came in she lifted up her face; there were tears there; but she smiled and said, "Well, William." I remember just enough to know that I was mad. The devil entered into me. I rushed into the kitchen, seized my gun, and deliberately shot her as she sat by that table. I am in prison for life, and have no desire to be released. If a pardon was offered me, I think I should refuse it. Buried here in this prison, I wait till the end comes. I trust God has forgiven me for Christ's sake. I have bitterly repented; I repent every day. Oh, the nights when in the darkness I see her face—see her just as she looked on me that fatal day! I shall rejoice when the time comes. I pray that I may meet her in heaven.' This was said with sobbings and tears that were heart-breaking to hear."

"There goes me but for the grace of God!" "What, is thy servant a dog, that he should do this great thing?" No! not a dog, but a young man or a young woman who is liable to forget that "small habits well pursued betimes may reach the dignity of crimes." If you do not measure your liquor with as much care as strong medicine; if you are not on your guard against those drinking habits of society and business which first draw, then drag, and then haul—beware lest tyrant custom make you a slave to what has been called "the most authentic incarnation of the principle of evil."

CHAPTER XII.

FURNISHING.

"By wisdom is a house built; by understanding it is established; and by knowledge the chambers are filled with all pleasant and precious treasures."—*Solomon's Practical Wisdom.*

"We cannot arrest sunsets nor carve mountains, but we may turn every English home, if we choose, into a picture which shall be no counterfeit, but the true and perfect image of life indeed."—*Ruskin.*

A condition of pleasantness in a house has a real power in refining and raising the characters of its inmates; so home should not only be a haven of rest, peace, and sympathy, but should have an element of beauty in all its details. Ugliness and discomfort blunt the sensibilities and lower the spirits. D'Israeli said, "Happiness is atmosphere," and from this point of view a few words about furnishing may not be out of place in our inquiry as to how to be happy though married. Certainly the fitting up and arranging of a home will not appear unimportant to those who think with Dr. Johnson that it is by studying little things that we attain the great art of having as little misery and as much happiness as possible. "Pound St. Paul's church into atoms and consider any single atom; it is, to be sure, good for nothing; but put these atoms together, and you have St. Paul's church. So it is with human felicity, which is made up of many ingredients, each of which may be shown to be very insignificant."

The expense of furnishing is often a source of considerable anxiety to young people about to marry. We think, however, that this matrimonial care is, or should be, much more lightly felt than in past years. Competition has made furniture cheaper, and it is now considered "bad form" to crowd rooms or to have in them the large heavy things that were so expensive. Elegance displayed in little things is the order of the day. A few light chairs of different sizes and shapes, a small lounge, one or two little tables, the floor polished round the edges and covered in the centre with a square of carpet, or, if the whole room be stained, with Oriental rugs where required; the windows hung with some kind of light drapery—what more do newly-married people require in their drawing-room? Oh! we have forgotten the piano, and we suppose it is inevitable, but it can easily be hired.

It is a great gain for a young couple to be compelled to economize, for, rich as they may become afterwards, habits of thrift never quite leave them. Their furniture may be scanty and some of it not very new, but common things can be prettily covered, and the dullest of rooms is set off by the knick-knacks that came in so plentifully among the bridal spoils. Besides, if they start with everything they want, there is nothing to wish for, and no pleasure in adding to their possessions. George Eliot has a subtle remark about the "best society, where no one makes an invidious display of anything in particular, and the advantages of the world are taken with that high-bred depreciation which follows from being accustomed to them."

No doubt there will be pictures and photographs, the hanging of which occasions considerable discussion, and perhaps involves the first serious divergence of opinion. We must remember, however, that it is much better to have no pictures than bad ones, and that photographs of scenery are rarely decorative. As regards one's relations when they are really decorative, even Mr. Oscar Wilde can see no reason why their photographs should not be hung on the walls, though he hopes that, if called on to make a stand between the principles of domestic affection and decorative art, the latter may have the first place.

It is a safe rule to have nothing in our houses that we do not know to be useful or think to be beautiful. We should show our love of art and beauty in our surroundings, and bring it to bear in the selection of the smallest household trifle. To have things tasteful and pretty costs no more than to have them ugly; but it costs a great deal more trouble. Simplicity, appropriateness, harmony of colour—these produce the best results. When we enter a room, the first feeling ought to be, "How comfortable!" and the second, as we glance quickly round to discover *why*, ought to be, "How beautiful!" Not a touch too much nor too little. The art is to conceal art. Directly affectation enters, beauty goes out. But while there should be nothing bizarre in our method of furnishing, rooms should reflect the individuality of their owners. They should never look as if they were furnished by contract. People should allow their own taste to have its way. Whatever we have, let it not be flimsy, but good of its kind. Good things are cheapest in the end, and it is economy to employ good dependable tradespeople.

When he heard of the occurrence of some piece of mischief, George the Fourth used to ask, "Who is *she*?" This question may be asked with much more reason when we enter a pretty room. Who is she whose judgment and fingers have so arranged these unconsidered trifles as to make out of very little an effect so charming? Compare a bachelor's house with the same house after its master has taken to himself a helpmate. "Bless thee, Bottom! bless thee! thou art translated!" the friends of his former state may well exclaim. Of course we are supposing the lady's head to be furnished, for if that do not contain a certain amount of common sense, good taste, and power of observation, the result will soon be observed in her house. A drawing-room should be for use and not for show merely, and should be furnished accordingly. It should be tidy, but not painfully tidy. Self-respect should lead us to have things nice in our homes, whether the eyes of company are to see them or not. It was surely right of Robinson Crusoe to make his solitary cave look as smart as possible. Who does not respect the wife whose dinner-table is prettily adorned with flowers even on days when no one but her husband has the honour of dining with her?

To furnish the kitchen is a troublesome and unsatisfactory business. It is unsatisfactory because one expends on kitchen utensils, which are rather dear, a considerable amount of money without having much to show. And it is troublesome to have to distinguish between the many implements a cook really does require and those which she only imagines to be necessary. Still, cook must be supplied with every appliance that is really necessary. Without these there may be an expenditure of time out of all proportion to her task. On the equipoise of that lady's temper depends to a not inconsiderable extent the comfort of the house. Have in the kitchen a good clock, and teach your servants to take a pleasure in making sweet and bright their own special chambers.

Our present sanitary ideas will tolerate no longer curtains on beds, or heavy carpets on the floors of sleeping apartments. Both foster dust, and dust conceals the germs of disease. That carpets are sometimes made a too convenient receptacle for dust is evident from the answer that was once given by a housemaid. Professing to have become converted to religion, she was asked for a proof of the happy change, and thus replied: "Now," she said, "I sweep *under* the mats." For bedrooms there should be narrow, separate, tight-woven strips of carpet around the bed and in front of furniture only. These are easy to shake, and in every sense in harmony with the simplicity and cleanliness which, if health is to be preserved, must pervade the bedroom. The more air it contains the better, and hence everything superfluous should be banished from it. But we shall not specify the different things which, in our opinion, should, or should not, be found in the several rooms of a house, for after all it is the arrangement of furniture rather than the furniture itself that makes the difference.

If the question be asked, Is it better to pick up furniture at auctions or to buy it in shops? we reply, Avoid auctions. Things are varnished up to the eye, and it is seldom possible to examine them. So you generally find on returning home from a sale that your purchases are by no means what they seemed.

As regards the expense of furnishing a small house such as young housekeepers of the middle class usually hire when first they settle down in life, this of course varies with circumstances, but even one hundred pounds ought nearly to suffice. To estimate the cost rightly, one should know the tastes of the people concerned, their social position, the size of their house, and the style of the locality in which they propose to live. Very good furniture can sometimes be obtained secondhand, but one must be on their guard against "bargains" that are worthless. There are certain articles, such as lamps, beds, and bedding, that should as a general rule be purchased new.

People are generally in too great haste when furnishing. They should be prudent, deliberate, and wait with their eyes open until they see the sort of things that will suit them. They should buy the most instantly necessary articles first with ready money, and add to these as they can afford it to carry out ideas formed by observation. They should buy what can be easily replaced after legitimate wear and tear, what their servants can properly attend to, and what will save labour and time.

CHAPTER XIII.

MARRIED PEOPLE'S MONEY.

"Never treat money affairs with levity—money is character."—*Sir E. Bulwer Lytton.*

A Scotch minister, preaching against the love of money, had frequently repeated that it was "the root of all evil." Walking home from the church one old person said to another, "An wasna the minister strang upon the money?" "Nae doubt," said the other, and added, "Ay, but it's grand to hae the wee bit siller in your hand when ye gang an errand." So too, in spite of all that love-in-a-cottage theorists may say, "it's grand to hae the wee bit siller" when marrying; unless, indeed, we believe that mortality is one of the effects of matrimony as did the girl, who, on meeting a lady whose service she had lately left, and being asked, "Well, Mary, where do you live now?" answered, "Please, ma'am, I don't live now—I'm married." To marry for love and work for silver is quite right, but there should be a reasonable chance of getting work to do and some provision for a rainy day. It is only the stupidity which is without anxiety, that complacently marries on "nothing a week; and that uncertain—very!" And yet such flying in the face of Providence is often spoken of as being disinterested and heroic, and the quiverfuls of children resulting from it are supposed to be blessed. As if it were a blessing to give children appetites of hunger and thirst, and nothing to satisfy them.

On the other hand, there is some truth in the saying that "what will keep one will keep two." There are bachelors who are so ultra-prudent, and who hold such absurd opinions as to the expense of matrimony that, although they have enough money they have not enough courage to enter the state. Pitt used to say that he could not afford to marry, yet his butcher's bill was so enormous that some one has calculated it as affording his servants about fourteen pounds of meat a day, each man and woman! For the more economical regulation of his household, if for no other reason, he should have taken to himself a wife.

Newly-married people should be careful not to pitch their rate of expenditure higher than they can hope to continue it; and they should remember that, as Lord Bacon said, "it is less dishonourable to abridge petty charges (expenses) than to stoop to petty gettings." That was excellent advice which Dr. Johnson gave to Boswell when the latter inherited his paternal estate: "You, dear sir, have now a new station, and have, therefore, new cares and new employments. Life, as Cowley seems to say, ought to resemble a well-ordered poem; of which one rule generally received is, that the exordium should be simple, and should promise little. Begin your new course of life with the least show, and the least expense possible; you may at pleasure increase both, but you cannot easily diminish them. Do not think your estate your own, while any man can call upon you for money which you cannot pay; therefore begin with timorous parsimony. Let it be your first care not to be in any man's debt."

The thrifty wife of Benjamin Franklin felt it a gala day indeed when, by long accumulated small savings, she was able to surprise her husband one morning with a china cup and a silver spoon, from which to take his breakfast. Franklin was shocked: "You see how luxury creeps into families in spite of principles," he said. When his meal was over he went to the store, and rolled home a wheelbarrow full of papers through the streets with his own hands, lest folks should get wind of the china cup, and say he was above his business.

Although the creeping in of luxury is to be guarded against at the commencement of married life, people should learn to grow rich gracefully. It is no part of wisdom to depreciate the little elegances and social enjoyments of our homes. Those who can afford it act wisely when they furnish their houses with handsome furniture, cover the walls with suggestive paintings, and collect expensive books, for these things afford refined enjoyment. One day a gentleman told Dr. Johnson that he had bought a suit of lace for his wife. *Johnson*: "Well, sir, you have done a good thing, and a wise thing." "I have done a good thing," said the gentleman, "but I do not know that I have done a wise thing." *Johnson*: "Yes, sir, no money is better spent than what is laid out for domestic satisfaction. A man is pleased that his wife is dressed as well as other people; and a wife is pleased that she is dressed."

We should be particular about money matters, but not penurious. The penny soul never, it is said, came to twopence. There is that withholdeth more than is meet, but it tendeth to poverty. People are often saving at the wrong place, and spoil the ship for a halfpenny worth of tar. They spare at the spigot, and let all run away at the bunghole.

She is the wise wife who can steer between penuriousness and such recklessness as is described in the following cutting from an American periodical. "My dear fellow," said Lavender, "it's all very nice to talk about economizing and keeping a rigid account of expenses, and that sort of thing, but I've tried it. Two weeks ago I stepped in on my way home Saturday night, and I bought just the gayest little Russian leather, cream-laid account-book you ever saw, and a silver pencil to match it. I said to my wife after supper: 'My dear, it seems to me it costs a lot of money to keep house.' She sighed and said: 'I know it does, Lavvy; but I'm sure I can't help it. I'm just as economical as I can be. I don't spend half as much for candy as you do for cigars.' I never take any notice of personalities, so I sailed right ahead. 'I believe, my dear, that if we were to keep a strict account of everything we spend we could tell just where to cut down. I've bought you a little account-book, and every Monday morning I'll give you some money, and you can set it down on one side; and then, during the week, you can set down on the other side everything you spend. And then on Saturday night we can go over it and see just where the money goes, and how we can boil things down a little.' Well, sir, she was just delighted—thought it was a first-rate plan, and the pocket account-book was lovely—regular David Copperfield and Dora business. Well, sir, the next Saturday night we got through supper, and she brought out that account-book as proud as possible, and handed it over for inspection. On one side was, 'Received from Lavvy, 50 dols.' That's all right! Then I looked on the other page, and what do you think was there? '*Spent it all!*' Then I laughed, and of course she cried; and we gave up the account-book racket on the spot by mutual consent. Yes, sir, I've been there, and I know what domestic economy means, I tell you. Let's have a cigar."

It is the fear of this sort of thing, and especially of extravagance in reference to dress, that confirms many men in bachelorship. A society paper tells us that at a recent dance given at the West-end, a married lady of extravagant habits impertinently asked a wealthy old bachelor if he remained single because he could not afford to keep a wife. "My innocent young friend," was the reply, "I could afford to keep three; but I'm not rich enough to pay the milliner's bills of one."

A wife who puts conscience into the management of her husband's money should not be obliged to account to him for the exact manner in which she lays out each penny in the pound. An undue interference on his part will cause much domestic irritation, and may have a bad influence on social morals.

In "Memoirs of the Life of Colonel Hutchinson," his wife says, "So liberal was he to her, and of so generous a temper, that he hated the mention of severed purses; his estate being so much at her disposal that he never would receive an account of anything she expended."

No one can feel dignified, free, and happy without the control of a certain amount of money for the graces, the elegant adornments, and, above all, for the charities of life. The hard-drawn line of simply paying the bills closes a thousand avenues to gentle joys and pleasures in a woman's daily life.

We would advise all wives to strike the iron when hot, so to speak, by getting their husbands, before the ardour of the honeymoon cools, to give them an annual allowance. The little unavoidable demands on a husband's purse, to which a wife is so frequently compelled to have recourse, are very apt to create bickering and discord; and when once good-humour is put out of the way, it is not such an easy matter to bring it back again.

A Chicago young lady, on being asked the usual question in which the words "love, honour, and obey" occur, made the straightforward reply: "Yes, I will, if he does what he promises me financially." The conduct of some husbands almost justified this answer.

As regards the important subject of Life Insurance there are few husbands and fathers who can afford to be indifferent to the possibility of making adequate and immediate provision for those dependent upon them, in case of their sudden removal.

This matter of Life Insurance should be settled before marriage, as well as all other monetary and legal arrangements that have to be made either with the wife that is to be, or with her relations, because post-matrimonial business details may introduce notes of discord into what might have been a harmonious home. "When I courted her, I took lawyer's advice, and signed every letter to my love—'Yours, without prejudice!'" It may not be necessary to be quite so cautious as the lover who tells us this; but he was certainly right in transacting his legal business before marriage rather than afterwards.

"Do not accustom yourself to consider debt only as an inconvenience; you will find it a calamity." Douglas Jerrold says that "the shirt of Nessus was a shirt not paid for." Those who would be happy though married must pitch their scale of living a degree below their means, rather than up to them; but this can only be done by keeping a careful account of income and expenditure. John Locke strongly advised this course: "Nothing," he said, "is likelier to keep a man within compass than having constantly before his eyes, the state of his affairs in a regular course of account." The Duke of Wellington kept an accurate detailed account of all the moneys received and expended by him. "I make a point," he said, "of paying my own bills, and I advise every one to do the same. Formerly I used to trust a confidential servant to pay them, but I was cured of that folly by receiving one morning, to my great surprise, dues of a year or two's standing. The fellow had speculated with my money, and left my bills unpaid." Talking of debt, his remark was, "It makes a slave of a man." Washington was as particular as Wellington was in matters of business detail. He did not disdain to scrutinize the smallest outgoings of his household, even when holding the office of President of the American Union.

When Maginn, always drowned in debt, was asked what he paid for his wine, he replied that he did not know; but he believed they "put something down in a book." This "putting down in a book" has proved the ruin of a great many people. The regular weekly payment of tradesmen is not only more honest, but far more economical. I know a wife who says that she cannot afford to get into the books of tradesmen, and who prides herself upon the fact that she will never haunt her husband after her death in the shape of an unpaid bill. These principles will induce married people to always try to have a fund reserved for sickness, the necessity of a change of abode, and other contingencies.

Perfect confidence as regards money matters should exist between married people. In a letter to a young lady upon her marriage, Swift says, "I think you ought to be well informed how much your husband's revenue amounts to, and be so good a computer as to keep within it that part of the management which falls to your share, and not to put yourself in the number of those polite ladies who think they gain a great point when they have teased their husbands to buy them a new equipage, a laced head, or a fine petticoat, without once considering what long score remained unpaid to the butcher."

With regard to keeping up appearances it must be remembered that few people can afford to disregard them entirely. A shabby hat that in a rich man would pass for perhaps an amiable eccentricity, might conceivably cause the tailor to send in his bill to a poorer customer. In this matter, as in so many others, we may act from a right or from a wrong motive. Nowhere is the attempt to keep up appearances more praiseworthy than in the case of those who have to housekeep upon very small incomes. The cotter's wife in Burns's poem who—

> "Wi' her needle and her sheers,
> Gars auld claes look amaist as weel's the new"—

deserves the title of heroine for her efforts to keep up appearances.

But the senseless competition that consists in giving large entertainments, the huge "meat-shows" which got under the name of dinner-parties, have no tendency to promote true happiness. Homes are made sweet by simplicity and freedom from affectation, and these are also the qualities that put guests at their ease, and make them feel at home. A Dublin lady took a world of trouble to provide a variety of dishes, and have all cooked with great skill, for an entertainment she was to give in honour of Dean Swift. But from the first bit that was tasted she did not cease to undervalue the courses, and to beg indulgence for the shortcomings of the cook. "Hang it," said Swift, after the annoyance had gone on a little, "if everything is as bad as you say, I'll go home and get a herring dressed for myself."

I once heard of a lady, who, not being prepared for the unexpected visitors, sent to the confectioner's for some tarts to help out the dinner. All would have gone off well, but that the lady, wishing to keep up appearances, said to the servant: "Ah! what are those tarts?" "Fourpence apiece, ma'am," was the reply.

There are thousands of women in these islands who cannot marry. But why can they not marry? Because they have false notions about respectability. And so long as this is the case, young men will do well to decline the famous advice, "Marry early—yes, marry early, and marry often."

"Why," asked a Sussex labourer, "should I give a woman half my victuals for cooking the other half?" Imagine the horror of this anti-matrimonial reasoner if it were proposed that he should give half his victuals for not cooking at all, or doing anything except keeping up appearances. "He was reputed," says Bacon, "one of the wise men that made answer to the question, when a man should marry? *A young man not yet, an elder man not at all.*" This answer would not appear so wise, if we had less erroneous notions on the subject of keeping up appearances.

CHAPTER XIV.

THE MANAGEMENT OF SERVANTS.

"A good mistress makes a good servant."—*Proverb.*

In England *materfamilias* is always complaining of servant difficulties. Those, however, who have lived in some of our colonies know that the very thought of an English servant conveys a certain soothing sensation to feelings that have been harassed by the servants—if we may so name such tyrants—in these places. A friend of mine in Bermuda wished to hire a nurse. One day, as she was sitting in her verandah, a coloured person appeared before her and suggested, laying great emphasis on the words in italics, "Are you the *woman* that wants a *lady* to nurse your baby?"

The servants in this and some other parts of the world consider themselves not merely equal but much superior to their employers, and there is a consequent difficulty in managing them. If you show any disinclination to their giving to friends much of the food with which you had hoped to sustain your family, they will disappear from your establishment without giving the slightest warning. A servant wishes to keep one or two members of her family in your house. If you dare to object, your widely-spread reputation for meanness will prevent any other servant applying for your situation for months. In a word, the employers of these helpful beings are every day reminded of the servant who said to his master: "I don't wish to be unreasonable, but I want three things, sir: more wages, less work, and I should like to have the keys of the wine-cellar."

Though matters are not quite so bad at home, there are nevertheless many much-tried masters and mistresses. Certainly some of them deserve to suffer. They have not given the very least attention to the art of managing servants. As parents spoil their children and wonder at the results, so do these masters and mistresses their servants. At one time they provoke them to anger about trifles, at other times they allow them to do as they like. Now they treat them with extreme coldness, on other occasions undue familiarity is permitted. In a word, they forget the fact that there is a common human nature between the kitchen and the parlour which must be admitted and well studied.

The ancient Romans, though they were heathen, and though with them servants meant slaves, included in the idea of *familia* their servants as well as their children. So, too, it was once amongst ourselves. Servants used to "enter the family," and share to some degree its joys and cares, while they received from it a corresponding amount of interest and sympathy. All this is changed. Servants are now rolling-stones that gather no moss either for themselves or their employers. They never dream of considering themselves members of the family, to stick to it as it to them through all difficulties not absolutely overwhelming. To them "master" is merely the man who pays, and "missis" the woman who "worrits." They think that they should change their employers as readily as their dresses, and never imagine that there could be between themselves and them any common interest. Only the other day I heard of a lady who had in one year as many as fourteen cooks! How could this mistress be expected to take any interest in or to consider herself responsible for the well-being of such birds of passage?

And yet surely the heads of a household are nearly as responsible for their servants as they are for their own children. We *are* the keepers of these our brothers and sisters, and are in a great measure guilty of the vices we tempt them to commit. A lady was engaged in domestic affairs, when some one rang the street-door bell, and the Roman Catholic servant-girl was bidden to say that her mistress was not at home. She answered, "Yes, ma'am, and when I confess to the priest, shall I confess it as your sin or mine?"

It is an unquestioned fact that many of the faults of servants are due to a want of due care on the part of their mistresses, who put up with badly-done work and make dishonesty easy by leaving things about.

If we want really good servants we must make them ourselves; so even from selfish motives we should do all we can to influence them for good. But it is much easier to mar than to make, and with servants the easiest way of doing this is to let them see that we are afraid of them. People spoil their servants from fear oftener than from regard. Some are afraid of the manner of their servants. They pass over many faults because they do not like the sulky looks and impertinent reply with which a rebuke is received.

Fifty years ago servants might be allowed to consider the warning of masters as a poor attempt at wit, as the Scotch coachman evidently did who, on being dismissed, replied, "Na, na; I drove ye to your christening, and I'll drive ye yet to your burial;" and the cook who answered in similar circumstances, "It's nae use ava gieing me warning; gif ye dinna ken when ye hae gotten a gude servant, I ken when I hae a gude master." As, however, servants are now seldom attached to a family by old associations they look upon the withdrawal of notice as a sign of weakness, and give themselves airs accordingly.

We should give our orders in a polite but firm manner, like one accustomed to be obeyed. It sometimes simplifies matters considerably to make a servant understand that she must either give in or go out. When fault has to be found, let it be done sharply and once for all, but nagging is dispiriting and intolerable. "Why do you desire to leave me?" said a gentleman to his footman. "Because, to speak the truth, I cannot bear your temper." "To be sure, I am passionate, but my passion is no sooner on than it's off." "Yes," replied the servant, "but it's no sooner off than it's on." Still we must never forget that the greatest firmness is the greatest mercy. Here is an illustration. The Rev. H. Lansdell tells us in his book "Through Siberia," that a Siberian friend of his had a convict servant, whom he had sent away for drunkenness. The man came back entreating that he might be reinstated, but his master said, "No; I have warned you continually, and done everything I could to keep you sober, but in vain." "Yes, sir," said the man; "but then, sir, you should have given me a good thrashing." Many a servant girl has gone to the bad because at some critical moment her mistress did not give her a good tongue-thrashing.

It cannot spoil tried servants to ask their opinion and advice on certain occasions, but we should not expect them to think for us altogether. To do this makes them as conceited as the Irish servant who replied to his master when that inferior being suggested his views as to the way some work should be done, "Well, sir, you may know best, but I know better!" Still, it is well to let servants know as often as we conveniently can the reason of our commands. This gives them an interest in their work, and proves to them that they are not considered mere machines. Never let a mistress be afraid of insisting upon that respect which her position demands. In turn she can point out that every rank in life has its own peculiar dignity, and that no one is more worthy of respect than a good servant. We should feel just as thankful to our servants for serving us, as we expect them to be for the shelter and care of the home which we offer them. There is a perfectly reciprocal obligation, and the manner of the employer must recognize it. "Whereas thy servant worketh truly, entreat him not evil, nor the hireling that bestoweth himself wholly for thee. Let thy soul love a good servant, and defraud him not of liberty." We have no right to every moment of a servant's time, and he or she will work all the better for an occasional holiday.

Those who feel that they are responsible for the character of their servants will endeavour to provide them with innocent amusements. When papers and books are read above stairs they might be sent down to the kitchen. If this were done, literature of the "penny dreadful" description would to a great extent be excluded.

Many employers behave as if the laws of good manners did not apply to their dealings with servants. Apparently they consider that servants should not be allowed any feelings. This was not the opinion of Chesterfield, who observes: "I am more upon my guard as to my behaviour to my servants, and to others who are called my inferiors, than I am towards my equals, for fear of being suspected of that mean and ungenerous sentiment of desiring to make others feel that difference which fortune has, perhaps too undeservedly, made between us." It is difficult, perhaps, to strike the exact mean between superciliousness and excessive familiarity, but we must make every effort to arrive at it. There is nothing more keenly appreciated by servants than that evenness of temper which respects itself at the same time that it respects others. A lady visited a dying servant who had lived with her for thirty years. "How do you find yourself to-day, Mary?" said her mistress, taking hold of the withered hand which was held out. "Is that you, my darling mistress?" and a beam of joy overspread the old woman's face. "O yes!" she added, looking up, "it is you, my kind, my *mannerly* mistress!"

Part of Miss Harriet Martineau's ideal of happiness was to have young servants whom she might train and attach to herself. In later life, when settled in a house of her own, she was in the habit of calling her maids in the evening and pointing out to them on the map the operations of the Crimean war, for she thought that young English women should take an intelligent interest in the doings of their country. Mrs. Carlyle was another tender mother-mistress to her servants, though her letters have made the world acquainted with the incessant contests which she was obliged to wage with "mutinous maids of all work" as Carlyle used to call them. "One of these maids was untidy, useless in all ways, but 'abounding in grace,' and in consequent censure of every one above or below her, and of everything she couldn't understand. After a long apostrophe one day, as she was bringing in dinner, Carlyle ended with, 'And this I can tell you, that if you don't carry the dishes straight, so as not to spill the gravy, so far from being tolerated in heaven, you won't be even tolerated on earth.'" It was better to teach the poor creature even in this rough way than not at all, that she ought to put her religion into the daily round and common tasks of her business; that

"A servant with this clause
Makes drudgery divine:
Who sweeps a room as for Thy laws
Makes that and the action fine."

So much of the comfort of home depends upon servants that a wise mistress studies them and values their co-operation.

"She heedeth well their ways,
Upon her tongue the law of kindness dwells,
With wisdom she dispenses blame or praise,
And ready sympathy her bosom swells."

She sees that their meals are regularly served, and that they are undisturbed during the time set apart for them. She does not think that any hole will do for a servant's bedroom. When caring for the children that they may have their little entertainments and enjoyments to brighten their lives, she includes the servants in the circle of her sympathies; and is always on the watch to make them feel that they are an integral part of the home, and that, if they have to work for it and to bear its burden, they are not excluded from a real share in its interests and joys. In a word, she feels for them and with them, and as a rule they do their best for her. That servants are not always ungrateful every good mistress is well aware. Among the inscriptions to the early Christian martyrs found in the catacombs at Rome there is one which proves that there were in those days, as no doubt there are now, grateful servants. "Here lies Gordianus, deputy of Gaul, who was murdered, with all his family, for the faith. They rest in peace. His handmaid, Theophila, set up this." Gentle, loving Theophila! There was no one left but thee to remember poor Gordianus, and perhaps his little children, whom thou didst tend.

In managing servants a little judicious praise is a wonderful incentive. The Duke of Wellington once requested the connoisseur whom the author of "Tancred" terms "the finest judge in Europe," to provide him a *chef.* Felix, whom the late Lord Seaford was reluctantly about to part with on economical grounds, was recommended and received. Some months afterwards his patron was dining with Lord Seaford, and before the first course was half over he observed, "So I find you have got the duke's cook to dress your dinner." "I have got Felix," replied Lord S., "but he is no longer the duke's cook. The poor fellow came to me with tears in his eyes, and begged me to take him back again, at reduced wages or no wages at all, for he was determined not to remain at Apsley House. 'Has the duke been finding fault?' said I. 'Oh no, my lord, I would stay if he had; he is the kindest and most liberal of masters; but I serve him a dinner that would make Ude or Francatelli burst with envy, and he says nothing; I go out and leave him to dine on a dinner badly dressed by the cookmaid, and he says nothing. Dat hurt my feelings, my lord.'"

On the vexed question of "visitors," mistresses might say to their servants, "When we stay in a lady's house, we cannot ask visitors without an invitation from our hostess, and we wish you to observe the same courtesy towards us. When we think it advisable, we will tell you to invite your friends, but we reserve to ourselves the right to issue the invitation; and if your friends come to see you, we expect that you shall ask our permission if you may receive them." A mistress who does not forget the time when she used to meet her affianced thus writes. "I always invite their confidence, and if I find any servants of my household are respectably engaged to be married, I allow the young men to come occasionally to the house, and perhaps on Christmas Day, or some festival of the kind, invite them to dine in the kitchen, and I have never yet found my trust misplaced. I should not like my own daughters only to see their affianced husbands out of doors, and, though the circumstances in the two cases differ materially, as a woman I consider we ought to enter into the feelings of those other women who are serving under us."

Half the domestic difficulties arise from a want of honesty among mistresses in the characters which they give each other of the servants they discharge. Many a servant receives flattering recommendations who does not deserve any better than the following: "The bearer has been in my house a year—minus eleven months. During this time she has shown herself diligent—at the house door; frugal—in work; mindful—of herself; prompt—in excuses; friendly—towards men; faithful—to her lovers; and honest—when everything had vanished."

It is often advocated that training-schools should be established for domestic servants, as a remedy to meet the domestic-servant difficulty. But improvement must begin at the head. If we are to have training-schools for domestic servants, the servants may very well say that there ought to be a training-school for mistresses. To rule well is even more difficult than to serve well.

The mistress then should learn how and when everything ought to be done, so that in the first place she can instruct, and, in the second, correct, if her orders be not carried out. If she does any of the household work herself, let it be to save keeping a servant, not to help those she has. The more you do in the way of help, the worse very often you are served. Let your servants understand that you also have your duties, and that your object in employing them is to enable you to carry on your work in comfort. So much have young women been spoiled by this system of auxiliary labour, that one cook who came to be engaged asked who was to fill her kitchen scuttle, as she would not do it herself. Mistresses must unite in the interest of the servants themselves, as much as in their own, to put down this sort of thing, for the demands have become so insolent, that, as a smart little maid once expressed it, "They're all wanting places where the work is put out."

CHAPTER XV.

PREPARATION FOR PARENTHOOD.

"If a merchant commenced business without any knowledge of arithmetic and book-keeping, we should exclaim at his folly and look for disastrous consequences. Or if, before studying anatomy, a man set up as a surgical operator, we should wonder at his audacity and pity his patients. But that parents should begin the difficult task of rearing children without ever having given a thought to the principles—physical, moral, or intellectual—which ought to guide them, excites neither surprise at the actors nor pity for their victims."—*Herbert Spencer.*

Whether as bearing on the happiness of parents themselves, or as affecting the characters and lives of their children, a knowledge of the right methods of juvenile culture—physical, intellectual, and moral—is a knowledge of extreme importance. This topic should be the final one in the course of instruction passed through by each man and woman, but it is entirely neglected.

"If by some strange chance," says Mr. Herbert Spencer, "not a vestige of us descended to the remote future save a pile of our school-books or some college examination papers, we may imagine how puzzled an antiquary of the period would be on finding in them no sign that the learners were ever likely to be parents. "This must have been the *curriculum* for their celibates," we may fancy him concluding: "I perceive here an elaborate preparation for many things, but I find no reference whatever to the bringing up of children." They could not have been so absurd as to omit all training for this gravest of responsibilities. Evidently, then, this was the school-course of one of their monastic orders."

Parents go into their office with zeal and good intentions, but without any better knowledge than that which is supplied by the chances of unreasoning custom, impulse, fancy, joined with the suggestions of ignorant nurses and the prejudiced counsel of grandmothers. "Against stupidity the gods themselves are powerless!" We all understand that some kind of preparation is necessary for the merchant, the soldier, the surgeon, or even for making coats and boots; but for the great responsibility of parenthood all preparation is ignored, and people begin the difficult task of rearing children without ever having given a thought to the principles that ought to guide them.

How fatal are the results! Who shall say how many early deaths of children and enfeebled constitutions, implying moral and intellectual weakness, are caused by ignorance on the part of parents of the commonest laws of life? Every one can think of illustrations.

Our clothing is, in reference to the temperature of the body, merely an equivalent for a certain amount of food, for by diminishing the loss of heat, it diminishes the amount of fuel needful for maintaining heat. Those parents cannot be aware of this who give their children scanty clothing in order to harden them, or who only allow a dawdling walk beside a grown-up person instead of the boisterous play which all young animals require and which would produce warmth.

Fathers who pride themselves on taking prizes at cattle-shows for their sheep and pigs are not at all ashamed never to ascertain the best kind of food for feeding children. They do not care if their children are fed with monotonous food, though change of diet is required for the preservation of health.

And then as to the intellects of children. Ignorance puts books into their hands full of abstract matter in those early years when the only lessons they are capable of learning are those taught by concrete objects. Not knowing that a child's restless observation and sense of wonder are for a few years its best instructors, parents endeavour to occupy its attention with dull abstractions. It is no wonder that few grown-up people know anything about the beauties and wonders of nature. During those years when the child should have been spelling out nature's primer and pleasurably exercising his powers of observation, grammar, languages, and other abstract studies have occupied most of his attention. Having been "presented with a universal blank of nature's works" he learns to see everything through books, that is, through other men's eyes, and the greater part of his knowledge in after life consists of mere words.

We are aware that it will provoke laughter to hint that for the proper bringing up of children a knowledge of the elementary principles of physiology, psychology, and ethics are indispensable. May we not, however, hold up this ideal of Mr. Herbert Spencer to ourselves and to others? "Here are," he says, "the indisputable facts: that the development of children in mind and body follows certain laws; that unless these laws are in some degree conformed to by parents, death is inevitable; that unless they are in a great degree conformed to, there must result serious physical and mental defects, and that only when they are completely conformed to can a perfect maturity be reached. Judge, then, whether all who may one day be parents should not strive with some anxiety to learn what these laws are." "I was not brought up, but dragged up," said the poor girl in the tale; and she touched unconsciously the root of nine-tenths of the vice and misery of the world.

Great as is the importance of some information, if children are to be properly reared, still knowledge is by no means all that preparation for parenthood should include. While Doctor Johnson was musing over the fire one evening in Thrale's drawing-room, a young gentleman suddenly, and, as Johnson seems to have fancied, somewhat disrespectfully, called to him: "Mr. Johnson, would you advise me to marry?" *Johnson* (angrily): "Sir, I would advise no man to marry who is not likely to propagate understanding."

Would the doctor have extended this restriction to all men and women who are not likely to propagate good bodies and souls? We know that there are people whose misfortunes and vices will spoil and ruin, not merely the lives of those they marry, but the lives of their children too. The miserable inheritance of their imperfections will be transmitted to coming generations. If it were only possible to keep all these people single, those who will be living thirty years hence would be living in a very different world from this.

The only restriction public opinion now puts to any marriage is that it should not be forbidden by the "Table of Kindred and Affinity" contained in the Prayer Book. When will all improvident marriages be equally illegal? When will scrofula, madness, drunkenness, or even bad temper and excessive selfishness be considered as just causes and impediments why parties should not be joined together in holy matrimony. Only the best men and women of this generation—could these be discovered—should become the parents of the next.

It has been flippantly asked why we should consult the interests of the next generation since the next generation has done nothing for us. The answer is plain. We have no right to bequeath to it an heritage of woe. Every man and woman can do much to make themselves worthy of the honour and responsibility of being a parent. Let them preserve their health, cultivate their social affections, and, above all, abstain from those sins which science and bitter experience assure us are visited on children. It is only when they do this that a new edition of themselves is called for.

> "Who is the happy husband? He
> Who, scanning his unwedded life,
> Thanks Heaven, with a conscience free,
> 'Twas faithful to his future wife."

And who are the happy parents? Those who, scanning their unwedded lives, thank Heaven they were faithful to future children.

It is to be hoped that few men now are as careless or as ignorant of consequences to children as was Mr. Tulliver in George Eliot's "Mill on the Floss," when he picked his wife from her sisters "o' purpose, 'cause she was a bit weak, like." We have come to see that, in order to be good mothers, women must be very unlike Mrs. Pullet in the same story, who was bent on proving her gentility and wealth by the delicacy of her health, and the quantity of doctor's stuff she could afford to imbibe.

But parents have not altogether given up sacrificing their own health and the health of their children to the Moloch of fashion. They have not quite ceased to burn incense to vanity. We have still to complain, as did Frances Kemble, that the race is ruined for the sake of fashion. "I cannot believe that women were intended to suffer as much as they do, and be as helpless as they are, in child-bearing; but rather that both are the consequences of our many and various abuses of our constitutions and infractions of God's natural laws. Tight stays, tight garters, tight shoes, and similar concessions to the vagaries of feminine fashion, are accountable for many of the ills that afflict both mother and child."

When King David was forbidden to build a temple for God's service because he had shed blood abundantly, with noble self-forgetfulness he laid up before his death materials with which Solomon his son might have the honour of building it. If parents would imitate his example and lay up the materials of good character and health, what glorious temples they might erect to God in the bodies, minds, and souls of their children!

CHAPTER XVI.

"WHAT IS THE USE OF A CHILD."

"A dreary place would be this earth
Were there no little people in it;
The song of life would lose its mirth
Were there no children to begin it.

"No babe within our arms to leap,
No little feet toward slumber tending;
No little knee in prayer to bend,
Our lips the sweet words lending.

"The sterner souls would grow more stern,
Unfeeling natures more inhuman,
And man to stoic coldness turn,
And woman would be less than woman.

"Life's song, indeed, would lose its charm,
Were there no babies to begin it;
A doleful place this world would be,
Were there no little people in it."—*John Greenleaf Whittier.*

When Franklin made his discovery of the identity of lightning and electricity, people asked, "Of what use is it?" The philosopher's retort was: "What is the use of a child? It may become a man!" This question—"What is the use of a child?" is not likely to be asked by our young married friends in reference to the first miniature pledge who is about to crown their wishes. They believe that one day he will become "the guardian of the liberties of Europe, the bulwark and honour of his aged parents." What a bond of union! What an incentive to tenderness! That husband has an unfeeling disposition who does not find himself irresistibly drawn by the new and tender tie that now exists.

I hope I appreciate the value of children. We should soon come to nothing without them. What is a house without a baby? It may be comparatively quiet, but it is very dull. A childless home misses its discipline and loses its music.

Children are *not* "certain sorrows and uncertain pleasures" when properly managed. If some parents taste the stream bitter it is very often they themselves who have poisoned the fountain. They treated their children when very young merely as playthings, humouring every caprice, and sacrificing to present fancies future welfare; then, when the charm of infancy had passed, they commenced a system of restraint and severity, and displayed displeasure and irritability at the very defects of which they themselves laid the foundation.

"In an evening spent with Emerson," says one who knew him, "he made one remark which left a memorable impression on my mind. Two children of the gentleman at whose house we met were playing in the room, when their father remarked, 'Just the interesting age.' 'And at what age,' asked Mr. Emerson, 'are children *not* interesting?'" He regarded them with the eye of a philosopher and a poet, and saw the possibilities that surround their very being with infinite interest. Each of his own children was for him a harbinger of sunny hours, an angel sent from God with tidings of hope.

Jeremy Taylor says, "No man can tell but he that loves his children how many delicious accents make a man's heart dance in the pretty conversation of those dear pledges; their childishness, their stammering, their little angers, their innocence, their imperfections, their necessities, are so many little emanations of joy and comfort to him that delights in their persons and society." And what shall be said of the man who does not love his children? That he, far more than the unmusical man—

"Is fit for treasons, stratagems, and spoils;
The motions of his spirit are dull as night,
And his affections dark as Erebus.
Let no such man be trusted."

"Civic virtues, unless they have their origin and consecration in private and domestic virtues, are but the virtues of the theatre. He who has not a loving heart for his child, cannot pretend to have any true love for humanity."

"I do not wonder," said Dr. Arnold, "that it was thought a great misfortune to die childless in old times, when they had not fuller light—it seems so completely wiping a man out of existence." "Write ye this man child-less." Cuvier's four children died before him. In his sixty-seventh year we find Moore writing, "The last of our five children is now gone, and we are left desolate and alone. Not a single relative have I left now in the world." How Hallam was successively bereaved of sons so rich in promise is well known. There is a touching gravestone in the cloisters of Westminster Abbey with the inscription, "Jane Lister, deare child, died Oct. 7, 1688." These parents knew only too well the value of a child.

A merchant in the city was accustomed to demand an excuse from his clerks whenever they arrived late. The excuse given, he invariably added, "Very well; but don't let it happen again." One morning a married clerk, being behind time, was promptly interrogated as to the cause. Slightly embarrassed, he replied, "The truth is, sir, I had an addition to my family this morning, and it was not convenient to be here sooner." "Very well," said the merchant, in his quick, nervous manner, "very well; but don't let it happen again."

There are people who think one, or, at most, two children, very well, but they don't wish it to happen again and again. So frequently do additions happen at Salt Lake City that nine families can, it is said, fill the theatre. One must love children very much to see the use of possessing the ninth part of a theatre-ful. And yet a family that is too small is almost as great an evil as one that is too large. It may be called a "large little family." Often an only child gives as much trouble as a large family. Dr. Smiles tells us that a lady who, with her husband, had inspected most of the lunatic asylums of England and the Continent, found the most numerous class of patients was almost always composed of those who had been only children, and whose wills had therefore rarely been thwarted or disciplined in early life.

What constitutes a large family? Upon this point there is much difference of opinion. A poor woman was complaining one day that she did not receive her proper share of charitable doles. Her neighbour Mrs. Hawke, in the next court, came in for everything and "got more than ever she was entitled to; for Mrs. Hawke had no family—not to speak of; only nine." "Only nine! how many then have you?" was the natural rejoinder. "Fourteen living," she replied. But even fourteen is not such a very large number when one is used to it. Some one is said to have begun a story of some trifling adventure which had befallen him with the words, "As I was crossing Oxford Street the other day with fourteen of my daughters"—Laughter followed, and the narrator never got beyond those introductory words. We do not believe this anecdote, but if it were true, was there not something heroic in the contented, matter-of-fact way in which the man spoke of his belongings? "Fourteen of my daughters!" An unsympathizing spectator might have said that any one with such a following ought to have been crossing not Oxford Street, but the Atlantic.

A nursery-maid was leading a little child up and down a garden. "Is't a laddie or a lassie?" asked the gardener. "A laddie," said the maid. "Weel," said he, "I'm glad o' that, for there's ower mony women in the world." "Heck, man," was the reply, "did ye no ken there's aye maist sown o' the best crap?" This rejoinder was more ready than correct, for as a matter of fact more boys are born than girls. It is natural for parents to desire offspring of both sexes. Both are required to complete a family. Being brought up together the boys acquire something of their sisters' delicacy and tact, while the girls learn something of their brothers' self-reliance and independence.

"Desire not a multitude of unprofitable children, neither delight in ungodly sons. Though they multiply, rejoice not in them, except the fear of the Lord be with them. Trust not thou in their life, neither respect their multitude: for one that is just is better than a thousand; and better it is to die without children, than to have them that are ungodly." In reference to children quality is far more to be desired than quantity. Without accepting pessimism, we may deny that the mere propagation of the human race is an object which presents itself as in itself a good. The chief end of man is not simply to have "the hope and the misfortune of being," but to glorify God and to serve humanity. What is the use of a child who is likely to do neither?

If it be the will of God to withhold offspring from a young couple, nothing should be said either by the husband or wife that could give the other pain on the subject. To do so is more than reprehensible; it is odious and contemptible. How unlike Elkanah, when, with sentiments at once manly and tender, he thus addresses his weeping wife—"Hannah, why weepest thou? and why eatest thou not? and why is thy heart grieved? am not I better to thee than ten sons?"

"We, ignorant of ourselves,
Beg often our own harms which the wise powers
Deny us for our good; so find we profit
By losing of our prayers."

Writing on this subject a lady tells us that she had a relation who was married some years without having a child. Her feelings partook not only of grief, but of anguish: at length, a lovely boy was granted her. "Spare, O God, the life of *my blessing*," was her constant prayer. Her blessing *was* spared: he grew to the years of manhood; squandered a fine fortune; married a servant-maid; and broke his mother's heart!

Another intimate friend of the author's was inconsolable for not having children. At length, the prospect of her becoming a mother was certain, and her joy was extreme. The moment of trial arrived: for four days and nights her sufferings and torture were not to be allayed by medical skill or human aid. At length her cries ceased; and, at the same moment that she gave birth to *two* children, she herself had become a corpse. "Give me children," said the impatient and weeping Rachel, "or else I die" (Gen. XXX. 1). Her prayer was heard, and in giving birth to her boy the mother expired.

Another impassioned mother, as she bent over the bed of her sick infant, called out, "Oh, no; I *cannot* resign him. It is impossible; I *cannot* resign him." A person present, struck with her words, noted them down in a daily journal which he kept. The boy recovered; and that day one-and-twenty years he was hanged as a murderer!

How terrible it is when a much-desired child is born to a comparatively useless existence by reason of some deficiency or deformity. Very touching is the story of a lady who, though deaf and dumb, became the wife of an earl through her beauty. In due course the king o' the world, the baby, presented himself—a fine child, of course, and a future earl. Soon after its birth, as the nurse sat watching the babe, she saw the countess mother approach the cradle with a huge china vase, lift it above the head of the sleeping child, and poise it to dash it down. Petrified with horror, wondering at the strange look of the mother's face, the nurse sat powerless and still; she dared not even cry out; she was not near enough to throw herself between the victim and the blow. The heavy mass was thrown down with a tremendous force and crash on the floor beside the cradle, and the babe awoke terrified and screaming, clung to his delighted mother, who had made the experiment to discover whether her child had the precious gift of voice and hearing, or was like herself, a mute.

In his "Bachelor's Complaint of the Behaviour of Married People," Charles Lamb speaks of "the airs which these creatures give themselves when they come, as they generally do, to have children. When I consider how little of a rarity children are—that every street and blind alley swarms with them—that the poorest people commonly have them in most abundance—that there are few marriages that are not blest with at least one of these bargains—how often they turn out ill and defeat the fond hopes of their parents, taking to vicious courses, which end in poverty, disgrace, the gallows, &c.—I cannot for my life tell what cause for pride there can possibly be in having them. If they were young phoenixes, indeed, that were born but one in a hundred years, there might be a pretext. But when they are so common——"

It is, however, far better for married people to take pride in their children than to be as indifferent to them as was a certain old lady who had brought up a family of children near a river. A gentleman once said to her, "I should think you would have lived in constant fear that some of them would have got drowned." "Oh no," responded the old lady, "we only lost three or four in that way."

What is the use of a child? Not very much unless its parents accept it, not as a plaything, much less as a nuisance, but as a most sacred trust—a talent to be put to the best account. It is neither to be spoiled nor buried in the earth—how many careless mothers do this literally!—but to be made the most of for God and for man. Perhaps there was only One who perfectly understood the use of a child. "Suffer the little children to come unto me, and forbid them not: for of such is the kingdom of God." In some lines to a child Longfellow has well answered the question we have been considering.

"Enough! I will not play the Seer;
I will no longer strive to ope
The mystic volume, where appear
The herald Hope, forerunning Fear,
And Fear, the pursuivant of Hope.
Thy destiny remains untold."

In the next chapter we shall point out how useful children are in educating their parents.

CHAPTER XVII.

THE EDUCATION OF PARENTS.

"O dearest, dearest boy! my heart
For better lore would seldom yearn,
Could I but teach the hundredth part
Of what from thee I learn."—*Wordsworth.*

"How admirable is the arrangement through which human beings are led by their strongest affections to subject themselves to a discipline they would else elude."—*Herbert Spencer.*

"My friend," said an old Quaker, to a lady who contemplated adopting a child, "I know not how far thou wilt succeed in educating her, but I am quite certain she will educate you." How encouraging and strengthening it should be for parents to reflect that, in training up their children in the way they should go, they are at the same time training up themselves in the way *they* should go; that along with the education of their children their own higher education cannot but be carried on. In "Silas Marner," George Eliot has shown how by means of a little child a human soul may be redeemed from cold, petrifying isolation; how all its feelings may be freshened, rejuvenated, and made to flutter with new hope and activity.

Very simple is the pathos of this matchless work of art. Nothing but the story of a faithless love and a false friend and the loss of trust in all things human or divine. Nothing but the story of a lone, bewildered weaver, shut out from his kind, concentrating every baulked passion into one—the all-engrossing passion for gold. And then the sudden disappearance of the hoard from its accustomed hiding-place, and in its stead the startling apparition of a golden-haired little child found one snowy winter's night sleeping on the floor in front of the glimmering hearth. And the gradual reawakening of love in the heart of the solitary man, a love "drawing his hope and joy continually onward beyond the money," and once more bringing him into sympathetic relations with his fellow men. "In old days," says the story, "there were angels who came and took men by the hand and led them away from the city of destruction. We see no white-winged angels now. But yet men are led away from threatening destruction; a hand is put into theirs which leads them forth gently towards a calm and bright land, so that they look no more backward, and the hand may be a little child's."

Children renew the youth of their parents and enable them to mount up with wings as eagles, instead of becoming chained to the rock of selfishness. We do not believe that "all children are born good," for it is the experience of every one that the evil tendencies of fathers are visited upon their children unto the third and fourth generation. Nevertheless all men are exhorted by the highest authority to follow their innocency, which is great indeed as compared to *our* condition who—

> "Through life's drear road, so dim and dirty,
> Have dragged on to three-and-thirty."

"Whosoever shall not receive the kingdom of God as a little child, he shall not enter therein." Evil tendencies are checked and good ones are educated or drawn out by children, for they call to remembrance—

> "Those early days, when I
> Shined in my angel-infancy,
> Before I taught my tongue to wound
> My conscience with a sinful sound,
> Or had the black art to dispense
> A several sin to every sense,
> But felt through all this fleshly dress
> Bright shoots of everlastingness."

When daily farther from the east—from God who is our home—we have travelled, children are sent to recall us or at least to make us long "to travel back, and tread again that ancient track."

Whatever we attempt to teach children we must first practise ourselves. Whatever a parent wishes his child to avoid he must make up his mind to renounce, and, on the other hand, if we leave off any good habit, we need not expect our children to continue it. Only the other day I heard a boy of five say to his father, "You must not be cross, for if you are, I shall be that when I grow up." "Mother," said a small urchin, who had just been saying his prayers at her knees; "Mother, when may I leave off my prayers?" "Oh, Tommy, what a notion! What do you mean?" "Well, mother, father never says his prayers, and I thought I was old enough to leave them off."

In young children the capacity for mimicry is very strong. They imitate whatever they see done by their elders. How wrong, then, is it for people to say or do before even a very young child what they would not say or do before an adult, supposed to be more observant! We must not say, "Oh, there's no one present but the child," for "the child" is reading, marking, and inwardly digesting character as it is exhibited in words, looks, and deeds. For the sake, then, of their children, if not for their own sakes, parents should seek to be very self-restrained, truthful, and, above all things, just. Right habits are imparted to children almost as easily as wrong ones.

The education of parents begins from the day their first child is born. A young man and woman may be selfish and egotistical enough until the "baby" comes as a teacher of practical Christianity into their home. Now they have to think of somebody beside themselves, to give up not a few of their comforts and individual "ways," for the one important thing in the house is King "Baby." If they really love their children, parents will become truthful in act as well as in word, knowing that truthful habits must be learned in childhood or not at all. They will be so just that "You'r' not fair" will never be rightly charged against them. And, as regards sympathy, they will try to be the friends and companions in sorrow and in joy as well as the parents of their children.

Nor is it only the moral nature that is developed in the school of parenthood. Even to attempt to answer the wise questions of children is a task difficult enough to afford healthy exercise to the greatest minds. When a child begins to cross-examine its parents as to why the fire burns, how his carte-de-visite was taken, how many stars there are, why people suffer, why God does not kill the devil—grown-up ignorance or want of sympathy too often laughs at him, says that children should not ask tiresome questions, and not only checks the inquiring spirit within him, but misses the intellectual improvement that would have come from endeavouring to answer his questions.

"Little people should be seen and not heard" is a stupid saying, which makes young observers shy of imparting to their elders the things that arrest their attention. Children would gladly learn and gladly teach, but if they are frequently snubbed they will do neither. Men such as Professor Robinson of Edinburgh, the first editor of the "Encyclopædia Britannica," have not been above receiving intellectual improvement and pleasure from a little child. "I am delighted," he wrote in reference to his grandchild, "with observing the growth of its little soul, and particularly with its numberless instincts, which formerly passed unheeded. I thank the French theorists for more forcibly directing my attention to the finger of God, which I discern in every awkward movement and every wayward whim. They are all guardians of his life and growth and power. I regret indeed that I have not time to make infancy and the development of its powers my sole study."

Some parents seem to imagine that they sufficiently perform their duty when they give their children a good education. They forget that there is the education of the fireside as well as of the school. At schools and academies there is no cultivation of the affections, but often very much of the reverse. Hence the value to the young of kindly home influences that touch the heart and understanding.

Among the poems of George Macdonald are the following pretty and playful lines called simply "The Baby"—

"Where did you come from, baby dear?
Out of the everywhere into here.
Where did you get your eyes so blue?
Out of the skies as I came through.
What makes your forehead smooth and high?
A soft hand stroked it as I went by.
What makes your cheek like a warm white rose?
I saw something better than any one knows.
Whence that three-cornered smile of bliss?
Three angels gave me at once a kiss.
Where did you get that coral ear?
God spoke, and it came out to hear.
Where did you get those arms and hands?
Love made itself into bonds and bands.
Whence came your feet, dear little things?
From the same box as the cherubs' wings.
How did they all first come to be you?
God thought about me, and so I grew.
But how did you come to us, you dear?
God thought about you, and so I am here.

Yes, God is thinking about our highest interests when He sends children to us. They are sent as little missionaries to turn us from evil and to develop within us the Divine image. When we see sin stirring in our children, no stroke seems too heavy to crush the noxious passion before it grows to fell dimensions and laughs to scorn the sternest chastisement. Heaven is saying to us, "Physician, heal thyself; strike hard, strike home; purge thine own heart of the evil. Lest your children should suffer, restrain your temper, curb your passions, master your unholy desires."

This, then, is one of the most important reasons why God "setteth the solitary in families." He desires not only that they should train up children in the nurture and admonition of the Lord, but also that they may by doing so be brought to Him themselves. When the day of account comes, after life's brief stormy passage is over, He wishes them to be able to say, "Here am I, for I have been educated by the children whom Thou hast given me."

CHAPTER XVIII.

WANTED!—MOTHERS.

> "There are comparatively very few women not replete with maternal love; and, by the by, take you care if you meet with a girl who '*is not fond of children*,' not to marry her *by any means*. Some few there are who even make a boast that they 'cannot bear children,' that is, cannot *endure* them. I never knew a man that was good for *much* who had a dislike to little children; and I never knew a woman of that taste who was good for anything at all. I have seen a few such in the course of my life, and I have never wished to see one of them a second time."—*Cobbett's "Advice to Young Men."*

Napoleon Buonaparte was accustomed to say that "the future good or bad conduct of a child depended entirely on the mother." In the course of a conversation with Madame Campan he remarked: "The old systems of instruction seem to be worth nothing; what is yet wanting in order that the people should be properly educated?" "Mothers," replied Madame Campan. The reply struck the emperor. "Yes!" said he, "here is a system of education in one word. Be it your care, then, to train up mothers who shall know how to educate their children."

"She who rocks the cradle rules the world," for she it is who guides and trains the opening minds of those who shall influence the coming generation. In its earliest years, the mother's every look, tone of voice, and action, sink into the heart and memory of her child and are presently reproduced in its own life. From this point of view the throne of motherhood ought, as Madame Lætitia Buonaparte believed, to take precedence of that of kings. When her son, on becoming an emperor, half playfully, half gravely offered her his hand to kiss, she flung it back to him indignantly, saying, in the presence of his courtiers, "It is your duty to kiss the hand of her who gave you life."

No wonder that a good mother has been called nature's *chef d'œuvre*, for she is not only the perfection of womanhood, but the most beautiful and valuable of nature's productions. To her the world is indebted for the work done by most of its great and gifted men. As letters cut in the bark of a young tree grow and widen with age, so do the ideas which a mother implants in the mind of her talented child. Thus Scott is said to have received his first bent towards ballad literature from his mother's and grandmother's recitations in his hearing long before he himself had learned to read. Goethe owed the bias of his mind and character to his mother, who possessed in a high degree the art of stimulating young and active minds, instructing them in the science of life out of the treasures of her abundant experience. After a lengthened interview with her a traveller said, "Now do I understand how Goethe has become the man he is." Goethe himself affectionately cherished her memory. "She was worthy of life!" he once said of her; and when he visited Frankfort, he sought out every individual who had been kind to his mother, and thanked them. The poet Gray was equally grateful to his mother. On the memorial which he erected over her remains he described her as "the careful, tender mother of many children, one of whom alone had the misfortune to survive her." In a corner of his room there was a trunk containing the carefully folded dresses of his dead mother, whom he never mentioned without a sigh.

When a mother once asked a clergyman when she should begin the education of her child, then four years old, he replied: "Madam, if you have not begun already, you have lost those four years. From the first smile that gleams upon an infant's cheek, your opportunity begins." Cowper's mother must have well used this opportunity considering the impression her brief companionship made upon the poet. She died when he was six years old, and yet in after-life he could say that not a week passed in which he did not think of her. When his cousin one day presented him with a portrait of his mother he said: "I had rather possess that picture than the richest jewel in the British crown; for I loved her with an affection that her death, fifty-two years since, has not in the least abated." Surely it is better for a mother to merit such love than to leave the care of her children almost entirely to servants because all her time is occupied "serving divers lusts and pleasures."

"Give your child to be educated by a slave," said an ancient Greek, "and instead of one slave, you will then have two." On the other hand, "happy is he whom his mother teacheth." One good mother is worth a hundred nurses or teachers. If from any cause, whether from necessity, or from indolence, or from desire for company, children are deprived of a mother's care, instruction, and influence, it is an incalculable loss.

Curran spoke with great affection of his mother, as a woman of strong original understanding, to whose wise counsel, consistent piety, and lessons of honourable ambition, which she diligently enforced on the minds of her children, he himself principally attributed his success in life. "The only inheritance," he used to say, "that I could boast of from my poor father, was the very scanty one of an unattractive face and person, like his own; and if the world has ever attributed to me something more valuable than face or person, or than earthly wealth, it was because another and a dearer parent gave her child a portion from the treasure of her mind."

Mrs. Wesley, the mother of John Wesley, made it a rule to converse alone with one of her little ones every evening, listening to their childish confessions, and giving counsel in their childish perplexities. She was the patient teacher as well as the cheerful companion of her children. When some one said to her, "Why do you tell that blockhead the same thing twenty times over?" she replied, "Because if I had told him only nineteen times I should have lost all my labour." So deep was the hold this mother had on the hearts of her sons, that in his early manhood she had tenderly to rebuke John for that "fond wish of his, to die before she died." It was through the bias given by her to her sons' minds in religious matters that they acquired the tendency which, even in early years, drew to them the name of Methodists. In a letter to her son, Samuel, when a scholar at Westminster, she said: "I would advise you as much as possible to throw your business into a certain *method*, by which means you will learn to improve every precious moment, and find an unspeakable facility in the performance of your respective duties." This "method" she went on to describe, exhorting her son "in all things to act upon principle;" and the society which the brothers John and Charles afterwards founded at Oxford is supposed to have been in a great measure the result of her exhortations.

The example of such mothers as Lord Byron's serves for a warning, for it shows that the influence of a bad mother is quite as hurtful as that of a good one is beneficial. She is said to have died in a fit of passion, brought on by reading her upholsterer's bills. She even taunted her son with his personal deformity; and it was no unfrequent occurrence, in the violent quarrels which occurred between them, for her to take up the poker or tongs, and hurl them after him as he fled from her presence. It was this unnatural treatment that gave a morbid turn to Byron's after-life; and, careworn, unhappy, great, and yet weak as he was, he carried about with him the mother's poison which he had sucked in his infancy. Hence he exclaims, in "Childe Harold"—

"Yet must I think less wildly:—I have though
Too long and darkly, till my brain became,
In its own eddy boiling and o'erwrought,
A whirling gulf of phantasy and flame:
And thus, *untaught in youth my heart to tame,*
My springs of life were poisoned,"

In like manner, though in a different way, the character of Mrs. Foote, the actor's mother, was curiously repeated in the life of her joyous, jovial-hearted son. Though she had been heiress to a large fortune, she soon spent it all, and was at length imprisoned for debt. In this condition she wrote to Sam, who had been allowing her a hundred a year out of the proceeds of his acting: "Dear Sam, I am in prison for debt; come and assist your loving mother, E. Foote." To which her son characteristically replied—"Dear mother, so am I; which prevents his duty being paid to his loving mother by her affectionate son, Sam Foote."

Mothers ought not to deceive themselves so far as to think that when they over-indulge their children they are exhibiting genuine mothers' love. In reality they are merely shifting their method of self-pleasing. We believe the love of God to be the supreme love; but have we ever reflected that in that awful love of God for His poor children of clay there must be mingled at once infinite tenderness and pity, and at the same time a severity which never shrinks from any suffering needed to recall us from sin? This is the ideal of all love towards which we should strive to lift our poor, feeble, short-sighted, selfish affections; and which it above all concerns a parent to strive to translate into the language of human duty. This is the truest love, the love which attaches itself to the very soul of the child, which repents with it, with tears bitterer than its own, for its faults, and, while heaping on it so far as may be every innocent pleasure, never for an instant abandons the thought of its highest and ultimate welfare.

The loving instruction of a mother may seem to have been thrown away, but it will appear after many days. "When I was a little child," said a good old man, "my mother used to bid me kneel down beside her, and place her hand upon my head while she prayed. Ere I was old enough to know her worth she died, and I was left too much to my own guidance. Like others, I was inclined to evil passions, but often felt myself checked and, as it were, drawn back by a soft hand upon my head. When a young man I travelled in foreign lands, and was exposed to many temptations; but, when I would have yielded, that same hand was upon my head, and I was saved. I seemed to feel its pressure as in the happy days of infancy; and sometimes there came with it a voice in my heart, a voice that was obeyed: 'Oh do not this wickedness, my son, nor sin against God.'"

With children you must mix gentleness with firmness. "A man who is learning to play on a trumpet and a petted child are two very disagreeable companions." If a mother never has headaches through rebuking her little children, she shall have plenty of heartaches when they grow up. At the same time, a mother should not hamper her child with unnecessary, foolish restrictions. It is a great mistake to fancy that your boy is made of glass, and to be always telling him not to do this and not to do that for fear of his breaking himself. On the principle never to give pain unless it is to prevent a greater pain, you should grant every request which is at all reasonable, and let him see that your denial of a thing is for his own good, and not simply to save trouble; but once having settled a thing hold to it. Unless a child learns from the first that his mother's yea is yea, and her nay nay, it will get into the habit of whining and endeavouring to coax her out of her refusal, and her authority will soon be gone.

Unselfish mothers must be careful not to make their children selfish. The mother who is continually giving up her own time, money, strength, and pleasure for the gratification of her children teaches them to expect it always. They learn to be importunate in their demands and to expect more and more. If the mother wears an old dress that her idle son may have a new coat, if she works that he may play, she is helping to make him vain, selfish, and good-for-nothing. The wise mother will insist upon being the head of her household, and with quiet unobtrusive dignity she will hold that place. She should never become the subject of her own children. Even in such mere external matters as dress and furniture her life should be better equipped. The crown should be on her head, not on theirs. Thus from babyhood they should be habituated to look up to, not down on, their mother. She should find time, or make it, to care for her own culture; to keep her intellectual and her art nature alive. The children may advance beyond her knowledge; let her look to it that they do not advance beyond her intellectual sympathies. Woe to both her and them if she does not keep them well in sight!

Happiness is the natural condition of every normal child, and if the small boy or girl has a peculiar facility for any one thing, it is for self-entertainment. One of the greatest defects in our modern method of treating children is to overload them with costly and elaborate toys, by which we cramp their native ingenuity or perhaps force their tastes into the wrong channel. The children of the humbler and the unpampered classes are far happier than are those children whose created wants are legion and require a fortune for their satisfaction.

Some mothers believe that they are exhibiting the proper "maternal feelings" in keeping their children at home when they should send them forth into the world, where alone they can be taught the virtue of self-dependence. A time will come when the active young man who is checked by foolish fondness will exclaim with bitterness—

> "Prison'd and kept, and coax'd and whistled to—
> Since the good mother holds me still a child,
> Good mother is bad mother unto me!
> A worse were better!"

Far more truly loving is the mother who sends her son into the battle of life preferring anything for him rather than a soft, indolent, useless existence. Such a mother is like those Spartan mothers who used to say to their sons as they handed to them their shields, "With it or upon it, my son!" Better death than dishonour was also the feeling of the mother of the successful missionary William Knibb. Her parting words to him were "William, William! mind, William, I had rather hear that you had perished at sea, than that you had dishonoured the Society you go to serve."

Never promise a child and then fail to perform, whether you promise him a bun or a beating, for if once you lose your child's confidence you will find it all but impossible to regain it. Happy is the mother who can say, "I never told my child a lie, nor ever deceived him, even for what seemed his good." Robert Hall once reproved a young mother because, in putting a little baby to bed, she put on her own nightcap, and lay down by it till it went to sleep. "Madam," said the eloquent preacher, "you are acting a lie, and teaching the child to lie." It was in vain that the mother pleaded that the child would not go to sleep. "That," said Hall, "is nonsense. Properly brought up it must sleep. Make it know what you want; obedience is necessary on its part, but not a lie on yours."

CHAPTER XIX.

"NURSING FATHERS."

"And kings shall be thy nursing fathers."—*Isaiah* xlix. 23.

It is an old saying, "Praise the child and you make love to the mother;" and it is a thing that no husband ought to overlook, for if the wife wish her child to be admired by others, what must be the ardour of her wishes with regard to *his* admiration! Cobbett tells us that there was a drunken man in his regiment, who used to say that his wife would forgive him for spending all the pay, and the washing money into the bargain, "if he would but kiss her ugly brat, and say it was pretty." Though this was a profligate he had philosophy in him; and certain it is that there is nothing worthy of the name of conjugal happiness unless the husband clearly evince that he is fond of his children.

Where you find children loving and helpful to their mothers, you generally find their father at the bottom of it. If the husband respect his wife the children will respect their mother. If the husband rises to offer her a chair, they will not sit still when she enters the room; if he helps to bear her burdens, they will not let her be the pack-horse of the household. If to her husband the wife is but an upper servant, to her children she will easily become but a waiting-maid. The first care of the true, wise husband will be to sustain the authority of the wife and mother. It must be a very remarkable exigency which allows him to sit as a court of appeal from her decisions, and reverse them. But although husbands ought not to vexatiously interfere with their wives in the management of children, especially of young children, still they must not shirk their share of care and responsibility. It was not without reason that Diogenes struck the father when the son swore, because he had taught him no better.

There is no effeminacy in the title "nursing fathers," but the contrary. Fondness for children arises from compassionate feeling for creatures that are helpless and innocent.

Napoleon loved the man who held with a steel hand, covered with a silk glove; so should the father be gentle but firm. Happy is he who is happy in his children, and happy are the children who are happy in their father. All fathers are not wise. Some are like Eli, and spoil their children. Not to cross our children is the way to make a cross of them. But, "Ye fathers, provoke not your children to wrath." That is, do not irritate them by unwise or capricious rules and ways. Help your wives to make the home lively and pleasant, so as to keep the children from seeking pleasure and excitement elsewhere. The proverb says that

"Clergymen's sons always turn out badly." Why? Because the children are surfeited with severe religion, *not* with the true religion of Christ, who was Himself reproved by the prototypes of such severe men.

"Where," asks Mr. James Payn, "is the children's fun? Boys are now crammed with knowledge like turkeys (but unfortunately not killed at Christmas), and there is absolutely no room in them for a joke." An idol called "success" is put up for worship, and fathers are ready to sacrifice the health and happiness of their children upon its altar. "The educational abomination of desolation of the present day," says Professor Huxley, "is the stimulation of young people to work at high pressure by incessant examinations." Some wise man (who probably was not an early riser) has said of early risers in general, that they are "conceited all the forenoon, and stupid all the afternoon." Now whether this is true of early risers in the common acceptation of the word or not, I will not pretend to say; but it is too often true of the unhappy children who are forced to rise too early in their classes. They are "conceited all the forenoon of life, and stupid all its afternoon." How much unhappiness might children be spared if fathers would goad them less, and sometimes cheer up that dulness which has fallen to most of us, by saying:

"Be good, dear child, and let who will be clever;
Do noble things—nor dream them all day long;
And so make life, death, and that vast for ever
One grand, sweet song."

What to do with our boys and girls is certainly a serious question, but the last thing we should do with them is to make them miserable. Why not disregard all false notions of gentility, and have each child well taught a manual trade? Then they will have riches in their arms, and you will have escaped the unpleasant alternative of the Jewish proverb, which says that he who does not teach his son a trade teaches him to steal.

We give here a sketch of Canon Kingsley as a father, because we do not remember any home life more beautiful and instructive. Because the Rectory-house was on low ground, the rector of Eversley, who considered violation of the divine laws of health a sort of acted blasphemy, built his children an outdoor nursery on the "Mount," where they kept books, toys, and tea things, spending long, happy days on the highest and loveliest point of moorland in the glebe; and there he would join them when his parish work was done, bringing them some fresh treasure picked up in his walk, a choice wild-flower or fern or rare beetle, sometimes a lizard or a field-mouse; ever waking up their sense of wonder, calling out their powers of observation, and teaching them lessons out of God's great green book, *without their knowing* they were learning. Out-of-doors and indoors, the Sundays were the happiest days of the week to the children, though to their father the hardest. When his day's work was done, there was always the Sunday walk, in which each bird and plant and brook was pointed out to the children, as preaching sermons to Eyes, such as were not even dreamt of by people of the No-eyes species. Indoors the Sunday picture-books were brought out, and each child chose its subject for the father to draw, either some Bible story, or bird or beast or flower. In all ways he fostered in his children a love of animals. They were taught to handle without disgust toads, frogs, beetles, as works from the hand of a living God. His guests were surprised one morning at breakfast when his little girl ran up to the open window of the dining-room, holding a long, repulsive-looking worm in her hand: "Oh, daddy, look at this *delightful* worm!"

Kingsley had a horror of corporal punishment, not merely because it tends to produce antagonism between parent and child, but because he considered more than half the lying of children to be the result of fear of punishment. "Do not train a child," he said, "as men train a horse, by letting anger and punishment be the *first* announcement of his having sinned. If you do, you induce two bad habits: first, the boy regards his parent with a kind of blind dread, as a being who may be offended by actions which to *him* are innocent, and whose wrath he expects to fall upon him at any moment in his most pure and unselfish happiness. Next, and worst still, the boy learns not to fear sin, but the punishment of it, and thus he learns to lie." He was careful too not to confuse his children by a multiplicity of small rules. "It is difficult enough to keep the Ten Commandments," he would say, "without making an eleventh in every direction." He had no "moods" with his family, for he cultivated, by strict self-discipline in the midst of worries and pressing business, a disengaged temper, that always enabled him to enter into other people's interests, and especially into children's playfulness. "I wonder," he would say, "if there is so much laughing in any other home in England as in ours." He became a light-hearted boy in the presence of his children. When nursery griefs and broken toys were taken to his study, he was never too busy to mend the toy and dry the tears. He held with Jean Paul Richter, that children have their "days and hours of rain," which parents should not take much notice of, either for anxiety or sermons, but should lightly pass over, except when they are symptoms of coming illness. And his knowledge of physiology enabled him to detect such symptoms. He recognized the fact, that weariness at lessons and sudden fits of obstinacy are not hastily to be treated as moral delinquencies, springing as they so often do from physical causes, which are best counteracted by cessation from work and change of scene.

How blessed is the son who can speak of his father as Charles Kingsley's eldest son does. "'Perfect love casteth out fear', was the motto," he says, "on which my father based his theory of bringing up children. From this and from the interests he took in their pursuits, their pleasures, trials, and even the petty details of their everyday life, there sprang up a friendship between father and children, that increased in intensity and depth with years. To speak for myself, he was the best friend—the only true friend I ever had. At once he was the most fatherly and the most unfatherly of fathers—fatherly in that he was our intimate friend and our self-constituted adviser; unfatherly in that our feeling for him lacked that fear and restraint that make boys call their father 'the governor.' Ours was the only household I ever saw in which there was no favouritism. It seemed as if in each of our different characters he took an equal pride, while he fully recognized their different traits of good or evil; for instead of having one code of social, moral, and physical laws laid down for one and all of us, each child became a separate study for him; and its little 'diseases au moral,' as he called them, were treated differently, according to each different temperament.... Perhaps the brightest picture of the past that I look back to now is the drawing-room at Eversley, in the evenings, when we were all at home and by ourselves. There he sat, with one hand in mother's, forgetting his own hard work in leading our fun and frolic, with a kindly smile on his lips, and a loving light in that bright gray eye, that made us feel that, in the broadest sense of the word, he was our father."

Of this son, when he was an undergraduate at Cambridge, his father (then Professor of History) writes: "Ah! what a blessing to be able to help him at last by teaching him something one's self!" And to a learned "F.G.S." he says very seriously: "My eldest son is just going off to try his manhood in Colorado, United States. You will understand, therefore, that it is somewhat important to me just now whether the world be ruled by a just and wise God, or by o. It is also important to me with regard to my own boy's future, whether what is said to have happened to-morrow (Good Friday) be true or false."

Writing to his wife from the seaside, where he had gone in search of health, he says: "This place is perfect; but it seems a dream and imperfect without you. Kiss the darling ducks of children for me. How I long after them and their prattle! I delight in all the little ones in the street, for their sake, and continually I start and fancy I hear their voices outside. You do not know how I love them; nor did I hardly till I came here. Absence quickens love into consciousness. Tell Rose and Maurice that I have got two pair of bucks' horns—one for each of them, huge old fellows, almost as big as baby."

Writing from France to "my dear little man," as he calls his youngest son (for whom he wrote the "Water Babies"), he says: "There is a little Egyptian vulture here in the inn; ask mother to show you his picture in the beginning of the bird-book." There was little danger that the sons of such a clergyman as this would turn out badly.

A companion picture of Dr. Arnold as a father, has been drawn by Dean Stanley: "It is impossible adequately to describe the union of the whole family round him, who was not only the father and guide, but the elder brother and playfellow of his children; the gentleness and tenderness which marked his whole feeling and manner in the privacy of his domestic intercourse. Enough, however, may perhaps be said to recall something at least of its outward aspect. There was the cheerful voice that used to go sounding through the house in the early morning, as he went round to call his children; the new spirits which he seemed to gather from the mere glimpses of them in the midst of his occupations—the increased merriment of all in any game in which he joined—the happy walks on which he would take them in the fields and hedges, hunting for flowers—the yearly excursion to look in the neighbouring clay-pit for the earliest coltsfoot, with the mock siege that followed. Nor, again, was the sense of his authority as a father ever lost in his playfulness as a companion. His personal superintendence of their ordinary instructions was necessarily limited by his other engagements, but it was never wholly laid aside. In the later years of his life it was his custom to read the Psalms and Lessons of the day with his family every morning; and the common reading of a chapter in the Bible every Sunday evening, with repetition of hymns or parts of Scripture by every member of the family—the devotion with which he would himself repeat his favourite poems from the Christian Year, or his favourite passages from the Gospels—the same attitude of deep attention in listening to the questions of his youngest children, the same reverence in answering their difficulties that he would have shown to the most advanced of his friends or his scholars—form a picture not soon to pass away from the mind of any one who was ever present. But his teaching in his family was naturally not confined to any particular occasions; they looked to him for information and advice at all times; and a word of authority from him was a law not to be questioned for a moment. And with the tenderness which seemed to be alive to all their wants and wishes, there was united that peculiar sense of solemnity, with which, in his eyes, the very idea of a family life was invested. The anniversaries of domestic events—the passing away of successive generations—the entrance of his sons on the several stages of their education, struck on the deepest chords of his nature, and made him blend with every prospect of the future the keen sense of the continuance (so to speak) of his own existence in the good and evil fortunes of his children, and to unite the thought of them with the yet more solemn feeling, with which he was at all times wont to regard 'the blessing' of 'a whole house transplanted entire from earth to heaven, without one failure.'"

What Luther was as a father may be imagined from a letter which he wrote when absent at the Diet of Augsburg, to his little boy, aged five years. The mother had written the home news, especially telling the loving father about his first-born, so to him, as well as to her, Luther wrote the following letter, full of fatherly fondness and charming naturalness.

"Grace and peace in Christ, my dear little boy. I am pleased to see that thou learnest thy lessons well, and prayest well. Go on thus, my dear boy, and when I come home I will bring you a fine fairing. I know of a pretty garden where are merry children that have gold frocks, and gather nice apples and plums and cherries under the trees, and sing and dance, and ride on pretty horses with gold bridles and silver saddles. I asked the man of the place whose the garden was, and who the children were. He said, 'These are the children who pray and learn and are good.' Then I answered, 'I also have a son, who is called Hans Luther. May he come to this garden, and eat pears and apples, and ride a little horse, and play with the others?' The man said, 'If he says his prayers, and learns and is good, he may come; and Lippus and Jost [Melanchthon's son Philip, and Jonas' son, Jodecus] may come, and they shall have pipes and drums and lutes and fiddles, and they shall dance, and shoot with little crossbows. Then he showed me a smooth lawn in the garden laid out for dancing, and there the pipes and crossbows hung. But it was still early, and the children had not dined, and I could not wait for the dance. So I said, 'Dear sir, I will go straight home and write all this to my little boy; but he has an aunt, Lene (great-aunt Magdalen) that he must bring with him.' And the man answered, 'So it shall be! go and write as you say.' Therefore, dear little boy, learn and pray with a good heart, and tell Lippus and Jost to do the same, and then you will all come to the garden together. Almighty God guard you. Give my love to Aunt Lene, and give her a kiss for me.—Your loving father, MARTIN LUTHER."

What is chiefly wanted in the education of children is a wise mixture of love and firmness. Parental authority should be regarded as vicegerent authority, set up by God and ruling in His stead. A parent is to a child what God is to a good man. He is the moral governor of the world of childhood. Parental government is therefore only genuine when it rules for the same ends as God pursues.

When children accord willing obedience the end of family government is gained. To attain this end a parent should be careful to observe the following rules. First, never to hamper a child with arbitrary restrictions, but, if possible, always to let the reasons of each command or prohibition be apparent; secondly, to let every punishment have some relation to the offence, and so imitate the great laws of nature, which entail definite consequences on every act of wrong; and, thirdly, never to threaten a punishment and afterwards shrink from inflicting it; finally, punishments should be severe enough to serve their purpose, and gentle enough to ensure the continuance of affection. Nor should the child be left alone until he feels that the punishment has been for his own good, and gives assurance of this feeling by putting on a pleasant face.

Human nature requires amusement as well as teaching and correction. One of the first duties of a parent is to sympathize with the play of his children. How much do little children crave for sympathy! They hold out every new object for you to see it with them, and look up after each gambol for you to rejoice with them. Let play-time and playthings be given liberally. Invite suitable companions, and do everything in your power to make home sweet. Authority, so unbent, will be all the stronger and more welcome from our display of real sympathy. If family government were well carried out in every home, children would be happier and better than they are now. Then there would be, even in our own great towns, a partial realization of the words of the prophet Zechariah, in reference to Jerusalem delivered: "And the streets of the city shall be full of boys and girls, playing in the streets thereof."

The home of our children ought never to be a prison where there is plenty of rule and order, but no love and no pleasure. We should remember that "he who makes a little child happier for an hour is a fellow-worker with God."

It was bitterly said of a certain Pharisaical household that in it "no one should please himself, neither should he please any one else; for in either case he would be thought to be displeasing God." This reminds us of the Scotchman who, having gone back to his country after a long absence, declared that the whole kingdom was on the road to perdition. "People," he said, "used to be reserved and solemn on the sabbath, but now they look as happy on that day as on any other." It is a blessed thing for the rising generation that such grotesque perversions of religion are seldom presented to them now; for every well-instructed Christian ought to be aware that religion does not banish mirth, but only moderates and sets rules to it.

CHAPTER XX.

POLITENESS AT HOME.

> "Manners are of more importance than laws. Upon these, in a great measure, the laws depend. The law teaches us but here and there, now and then. Manners are what vex or soothe, corrupt or purify, exalt or debase, barbarize or refine us, by a constant, steady, uniform, insensible operation, like that of the air we breathe in. They give their whole form and colour to our lives. According to their quality, they aid morals, they supply laws, or they totally destroy them."—*Burke.*

About twelve thousand police in London are able to take care of about four million people. How is it done? Chiefly by moral force, and, above all, by civility. Sir Edmund Henderson, the Chief Commissioner of the force, said on a recent occasion that it was by "strict attention to duty, by sobriety, and, above all, by civility," that the police endeavoured to do their duty. "I lay great stress upon civility," said the Chief Commissioner, "for I think it is the great characteristic of the metropolitan police force."

If civility and politeness have such an influence upon the hard, rough world of London how much greater will be the effect of good manners or beautiful behaviour, not only in rendering comparatively safe the many difficult crossings in the path of newly-married people, but also in adorning even the smallest details of family life! True courtesy exhibits itself in a disposition to contribute to the happiness of others, and in refraining from all that may annoy them. And the cultivation day by day of this sweet reasonableness is almost as necessary to the comfort of those who live together as the daily calls of the milkman and the baker. If no two people have it so much in their power to torment each other as husband and wife, it is their bounden duty to guard against this liability by cultivating the habit of domestic politeness. It is a mistake to suppose that the forms of courtesy can be safely dispensed with in the family circle. With the disappearance of the forms the reality will too often disappear. The very effort of appearing bright under adverse circumstances is sure to render cheerfulness easier on another occasion.

Good manners like good words cost little and are worth much. They oil the machinery of social life, but more especially of domestic life. If a cheerful "good morning" and "good evening" conciliate strangers they are not lost upon a wife. Hardness and repulsiveness of manner originate in want of respect for the feelings of others.

"Remember," says Sydney Smith, "that your children, your wife, and your servants have rights and feelings; treat them as you would treat persons who could turn again. Do not attempt to frighten children and inferiors by passion; it does more harm to your own character than it does good to them. Passion gets less and less powerful after every defeat. Husband energy for the real demand which the dangers of life make upon it." Good manners are more than "surface Christianity." Rowland Hill was right when he said, "I do not think much of a man's religion unless his dog and cat are the happier for it."

"Woman was made out of a rib from the *side* of Adam—not out of his head to top him, not out of his feet to be trampled on by him, but out of his side to be equal to him: under his arm to be protected, and near his heart to be loved."

"Use the woman tenderly, tenderly;
From a crooked rib God made her slenderly:
Straight and strong He did not make her,
So if you try to bend you'll break her."

Men are cautioned by the Jewish Talmud to be careful lest they cause women to weep, "for God counts their tears."

There are some people who stretch their manners to such an unnatural degree in society that they are pretty sure to go to the opposite extreme when relaxing at home. Feeling released from something that was hanging over them they run wild and become rude in consequence of their late restraint.

Is it not, to say the least, probable that such patient humility as the following would be followed by a reaction? Bishop Thirlwall was generally regarded, except by the small circle of those who knew him intimately, with much awe by his clergy, who thought that they had better keep as far as possible out of the way of their terribly logical and rather sarcastic diocesan. The legend was that he had trained a highly sagacious dog into the habit of detecting and biting intrusive curates. An amusing story is told of a humble-minded Levite who was staying at Abergwili Palace on the occasion of an ordination. An egg was placed before him, which, on tapping, proved a very bad one indeed. The Bishop made a kindly apology, and told a servant to bring a fresh one. "No, thank you, my lord," replied the young clergyman, with a penitential expression of countenance; "it is quite good enough for me."

We think that the clergyman's wife would have acted rashly if, soon after this occurrence, *she* should have tried the patience of her Job with an antiquated egg.

The proverb "familiarity breeds contempt" suggests another reason why the manners displayed at home are not, generally speaking, as good as they should be.

There is generally greater harmony when a husband's duties necessitate his remaining several hours of the day from home. "For this relief, much thanks!" will be the not unnatural sentiment of a grateful wife. And to the husband, on his return, home will appear far sweeter than if he had idled about the house all day with nothing to do but torment his wife. Richter says that distance injures love less than nearness. People are more polite when they do not see too much of each other.

Madam! no gentleman is entitled to such distinguished consideration as your husband. Sir! no lady is entitled to such deferential treatment as your wife.

Awkward consequences that could not have been foreseen have sometimes followed domestic rudeness. It is related of Lord Ellenborough that, when on one occasion he was about to set out on circuit, his wife expressed a wish to accompany him; a proposition to which his lordship assented, provided there were no bandboxes tucked under the seat of his carriage, as he had too often found there had been when honoured with her ladyship's company before. Accordingly they both set out together, but had not proceeded very far before the judge, stretching out his legs under the seat in front of him, kicked against one of the flimsy receptacles which he had specially prohibited. Down went the window with a bang and out went the bandbox into the ditch. The startled coachman immediately commenced to pull up, but was ordered to drive on and let the thing lie where it was. They reached the assize town in due course, and his lordship proceeded to robe for the court. "And now, where's my wig?—where's my wig?" he demanded, when everything else had been donned. "Your wig, my lord," replied the servant, tremulously, "was in that bandbox your lordship threw out of the window as we came along."

Sir Robert Walpole used to say that he never despaired of making up a quarrel between women unless one of them had called the other old or ugly. In the same way married people need not despair of realizing truly united and therefore happy lives if they will only study each other's weak points, as skaters look out for the weak parts of the ice, in order to keep off them.

Nothing is more unmanly as well as unmannerly than for a husband to speak disparagingly of either his wife or of the marriage state before strangers. Lord Erskine once declared at a large party that "a wife was a tin canister tied to one's tail;" upon which Sheridan, who was present when the remark was made, presented to Lady Erskine the following lines:

"Lord Erskine, at woman presuming to rail,
Calls a wife a tin canister tied to one's tail;
And fair Lady Anne, while the subject he carries on,
Seems hurt at his lordship's degrading comparison.

But wherefore degrading? Considered aright,
A canister's polished and useful and bright;
And should dirt its original purity hide,
That's the fault of the puppy to whom it is tied."

The "puppy" only got what he deserved.

When a husband happens to be a mere goose, happy if only a goose, though he may keep up the delusion that he is the "head of the family," it becomes the wife's duty to exercise real control. But she may be a responsible Prime Minister without usurping, much less parading, the insignia of Royalty. And if she have the feelings of a gentlewoman she will not allow every one to *see* the reins of government in her hand as did a colonel's wife known to me, of whom even the privates and drummer boys in her husband's (?) regiment used to say: "Mrs. ——, she's the colonel." What Burke said of his wife's eyes describe woman's proper place in the domestic Cabinet: "Her eyes have a mild light, but they awe when she pleases; they command, like a good man out of office, not by authority, but by virtue." Too often it is the poor wife who has to bear the heaviest part of the burdens of domestic life while the unchivalrous husband struts before as head of the house quite unencumbered.

Even the youngest child may claim to be treated with politeness. "I feel," said President Garfield, "a profounder reverence for a boy than for a man. I never meet a ragged boy in the street without feeling that I may owe him a salute, for I know not what possibilities may be buttoned up under his coat." Fathers should look upon their children with respect, for he who is "only a child" may become a much better and greater man than his father.

Without spoiling our children we should make their lives as pleasant as we possibly can, always remembering that the poor things never asked to be born, and that they may "not long remain." The boy dies perhaps at the age of ten or twelve. Of what *use* then all the restraints, all the privations, all the pain, that you have inflicted upon him? He falls, and leaves your mind to brood over the possibility of your having abridged a life so dear to you.

For good and for evil home is a school of manners. Children reflect, as in a mirror, not only the general habits and characters of their parents, but even their manner of gesture and of speech. "A fig-tree looking on a fig-tree becometh fruitful." If "a gentleman always a gentleman" and "a lady always a lady" are the examples set by papa and mamma, the children will take them in almost through the pores of the skin.

"For the child," says Richter, "the most important era of life is that of childhood, when he begins to colour and mould himself by companionship with others. Every new educator affects less than his predecessor, until at last, if we regard all life as an educational institution, a circumnavigator of the world is less influenced by all the nations he has seen than by his nurse."

CHAPTER XXI.

SUNSHINE.

"Love is sunshine."—*Longfellow.*

"God wishes us to have sunlight in our homes. He would have in them a tender play of laughter and humour, a pleasant interchange of light and colour and warmth, in word and mirth, which makes the brightness perfect, and is as much the work of the sunlight in the house, as the delightful gaiety of nature is the doing of the sun."—*Stopford Brooke.*

It is a comparatively easy thing to preserve a cheerful appearance when away from home, or even to present a brave front to meet the great emergencies of life. And yet the most genial-hearted of diners-out may be a domestic bully in the privacy of his own household; and the hero who has faced a battery without shrinking may be unable to take a cup of lukewarm coffee from his wife's hands without a grumble. The real happiness of a home depends upon a determination to lay no undue stress upon little matters, and a resolve to hold one's own irritability in constant check. For it is the sum of trivial affairs that make up the day's account, and it is the—

"Cares that *petty shadows* cast,
By which our lives are chiefly proved."

True home sunshine, if it consistently brighten the features of one member in a family, is pretty sure to be reflected from the faces of the rest.

"I thought," said a father, the other day, "as I sat in the railway carriage on my way home, of my impatience with the members of my family, and I felt ashamed. As soon as they are out of my sight I see clearly where my mistakes are; but when they are around me I forget my good resolutions."

It is quite true that the dear ones at home are more to us than Kings and Queens, than House of Lords or House of Commons, than the mightiest and noblest in the world. And yet we often treat them worse than we treat strangers. With others, whom we meet in business or in society, we are half unconsciously on our guard. Hasty words are repressed, and frowns are banished. But the dear ones at home usually have the pleasure or the pain of seeing us precisely as we are in the mood of the moment. To their sorrow we "make no strangers" of them. If our nerves are overstrung, or our tempers tried, so far from endeavouring to conceal the fact we make them feel it. The hero in great crises may be moved by the pressure of small annoyances to throw a boot at his *valet de chambre*, or to snarl at his wife. Individually these faults of temper may be small, but so are the locusts that collectively conceal the sun. "Only perfection can bear with imperfection." The better a man becomes the more allowance will he make for the shortcomings of others.

In order to have sunlight at home, it is not enough negatively to abstain from fault-finding and general peevishness. We should recognize praise as a positive duty. If a thing is done wrongly, better sometimes to say nothing about it. Wait until it happens to be done rightly, and then give marked praise. The third time, the charm of your approbation will produce a much better performance. If it is possible to "damn with faint praise," how much more damaging must be—no praise at all. How much potential goodness and greatness would become actual but for the wet blanket of sullen silence! "As we must account for every idle word, so we must for every idle silence." This saying of Franklin should suggest speech in season to ungrateful husbands who never throw a word of encouragement to their wives however deserving. In military riding schools may often be heard the command—"Make much of your horses!" The horses have been trotting, galloping, and jumping. They have had to stand quietly while the men dismounted and fired their carbines kneeling before them. They have gone through their parts well, so after the men have again mounted, the order is given—"Make much of your horses!" and all the riders pat simultaneously the proudly-arched necks of their deserving steeds. Husbands, take the hint and make much of your wives!

We may here introduce some words of Miss Cobbe in reference to the moral atmosphere of the house, which depends so immensely on the tone of the mistress. "I conceive that good, and even high animal spirits are among the most blessed of possessions—actual wings to bear us up over the dusty or muddy roads of life; and I think that to keep up the spirits of a household is not only indefinitely to add to its happiness, but also to make all duties comparatively light and easy. Thus, however naturally depressed a mistress may be, I think she ought to struggle to be cheerful, and to take pains never to quench the blessed spirits of her children or guests. All of us who live long in great cities get into a sort of subdued-cheerfulness tone. We are neither very sad nor very glad; we neither cry, nor ever enjoy that delicious experience of helpless laughter, the *fou rira* which is the joy of youth. I wish we could be more really light of heart." We all share this wish; but how is it to be realized? By living simple, well-regulated lives, and by casting all our anxiety upon God who careth for us.

Professor Blaikie commences a paper on "How to Get Rid of Trouble," by saying that once he had occasion to call on the chief of the constabulary force in one of our largest cities. "The conversation having turned on the arrangements for extinguishing fire, the chief constable entered with great alacrity into the subject, and after some verbal explanations, added, 'If you can spare half an hour, I will call out my men, and you shall see how we proceed.' I was taken aback at the idea of the firemen and engines being called out on a fine summer day to let a stranger see them at work; so I thanked him for his offer, but added that I could not think of giving him so much trouble. 'Trouble!' said he; 'what's that? That's a word I don't know.' 'You are a happy man,' was the reply, 'if you don't know the meaning of trouble.' 'No, indeed,' he said. 'I assure you I do not. The word is not in my dictionary.' As I was still incredulous, and wondering whether or not he had lost his senses, he rang the bell, and bade his clerk fetch him an English dictionary. Handing it to me, he said, 'Now, sir, please look and see whether you can find the word "trouble."' I turned to the proper place, and there, to be sure, where the word had been, I found it carefully erased by three lines of red ink. Of course I caught the idea at once. In a great work like that of the police in such a place, trouble was never to be thought of. No inroad that might be required on the ease, or the sleep, or the strength of any member of the force was ever to be grudged on the score that it was too much trouble. In the work of that office the thought of trouble was to be unknown. I felt that I had got a sermon from the chief of police, and a notable sermon, too. The three lines of red ink were as clear and telling as any three heads into which I had ever divided my discourse. It was a thrilling sermon, too—it set something vibrating within me."

This incident refers to trouble in the active sense; but even trouble in the sense of sorrow and disappointment may be to a large extent effaced from the family circle by certain red lines. Here is one of them. *Do not make the trouble worse than it really is.* Rather let us resolve to look at the bright side of things. If we had nothing more to think of, the proverbs that have been coined in the mint of hope ought to encourage us. "Nothing so bad but it might have been worse;" "'Tis always morning somewhere in the world;" "When things are at the worst they mend;" "The darkest hour of night is that which precedes the dawn." Let us try to form the habit of thinking how much there is to cheer us even when there may be much to depress; how often, on former occasions of trouble, we have been wonderfully helped; how foolish it is to anticipate evil before it comes.

"How dismal you look!" said a bucket to his companion, as they were going to the well. "Ah!" replied the other, "I was reflecting on the uselessness of our being filled, for let us go away ever so full, we always come back empty." "Dear me! how strange to look at it in that way!" said the other bucket. "Now I enjoy the thought that however *empty* we come, we always go away *full*. Only look at it in that light, and you will be as cheerful as I am."

Another red line which effaces trouble is *patience*. Speaking of the cheerful submission and trust of the London poor a well-known clergyman says: "Come with me; turn under this low doorway; climb these narrow creaking stairs; knock at the door. A pleasant voice bids you enter. You see a woman sixty-four years of age, her hands folded and contracted, her whole body crippled and curled together, as cholera cramped, and rheumatism fixed it twenty-eight years ago. For sixteen years she has not moved from her bed, nor looked out of the window; and has been in constant pain, while she cannot move a limb. Listen—she is thankful. For what? For the use of one thumb; with a two-pronged fork, fastened to a stick, she can turn over the leaves of an old-fashioned Bible, when placed within her reach. Hear her: 'I'm content to lie here as long as it shall please Him, and to go when He shall call me.'"

The third red line we would suggest is—*Try to get good out of your troubles.* Undoubtedly it is to be got, if the right way be taken to extract it. Scarcely any loss is without compensation. How often has the dignity of self-support and self-respect been gained when an external prop has been removed! How often have we been eventually glad that our wishes were not fulfilled! Plato tells us that "just penalties are the best gifts of the gods," and Goethe said he never had an affliction that he did not turn into a poem. The daylight must fade before we can behold the shining worlds around us, and the rigour of winter must be endured before our hearts can thrill with delight at the approach of Spring.

For the sake of household sunshine we should endeavour to keep in health. Lowness of tone, nervous irritability, the state of being ill-at-ease—these and many other forms of ill-health may, as a general rule, be avoided by those who endeavour to preserve their health as a sacred duty. If most people have but little health, it is because they transgress the laws of nature, alternately stimulating and depressing themselves. For our own sake and for the sake of others whom we trouble by irritability, we are bound to obey these laws—fresh air, exercise, moderate work, conquest of appetite.

"The deception," says Sydney Smith, "as practised upon human creatures, is curious and entertaining. My friend sups late; he eats some strong soup, then a lobster, then some tart, and he dilutes these esculent varieties with wine. The next day I call upon him. He is going to sell his house in London, and to retire into the country. He is alarmed for his eldest daughter's health. His expenses are hourly increasing, and nothing but a timely retreat can save him from ruin. All this is the lobster: and when over-excited nature has had time to manage this testaceous encumbrance, the daughter recovers, the finances are in good order, and every rural idea effectually excluded from the mind. In the same manner old friendships are destroyed by toasted cheese, and hard, salted meat has led to suicide. Unpleasant feelings of the body produce correspondent sensations in the mind, and a great scene of wretchedness is sketched out by a morsel of indigestible and misguided food. Of such infinite consequence to happiness is it to study the body!"

On the other hand, "A merry heart doeth good like a medicine." We should "laugh and be well," as enjoined by an old English versifier.

"To cure the mind's wrong bias, spleen,
Some recommend the bowling-green;
Some, hilly walks; all, exercise;
Fling but a stone, the giant dies;
Laugh and be well. Monkeys have been
Extreme good doctors for the spleen;
And kitten, if the humour hit,
Has harlequined away the fit."

It is the bounden duty of those who live together to cultivate the sunny side of life. To rejoice with those who rejoice is as much a duty as to weep with those that weep. Many have not that "great hereditary constitutional joy" which springs from a natural genius for happiness, but all may at least try to add to the stock of the household's cheerfulness. It is about the most useful contribution that any member of a family can make.

"As, although in the season of rainstorms and showers,
The tree may strike deeper its roots;
It needs the warm brightness of sunshiny hours,
To ripen the blossoms and fruits."

Sunlike pleasures never shine in idle homes. If a useful occupation or innocent hobby be not provided for the several members of a family, they are sure to spend their time in maliciously tormenting each other.

Those whose only care in life is to avoid care make a great mistake. They forget that even roses have thorns, and that pleasure is appreciated and enjoyed for its variety and contrast to pain. After all there is but one way of producing sunshine in our homes. We must first let the light into our own souls, and then like burning glasses we shall give it out to others, but especially to those of our own household. And whence comes the soul's calm sunshine and joy in right doing but from the Sun of Righteousness?

If there are many unhappy homes, many wretched families—more by far than is generally supposed—what is the cure for this? "Sweet reasonableness" as taught by Jesus Christ. If we would let Him into our houses to dwell with us, and form one of our family circle, He would turn our homes into little Edens.

CHAPTER XXII.

THEY HAD A FEW WORDS.

"Something light as air—a look,
A word unkind or wrongly taken—
Oh, love, that tempests never shook,
A breath, a touch like this hath shaken,
And ruder words will soon rush in
To spread the breach that words begin."—*Moore.*

"Married life should be a sweet, harmonious song, and, like one of Mendelssohn's, 'without *words*.'"—*Judy.*

When the sunshine of domestic bliss has become more or less clouded by quarrels between a husband and wife, observers very often describe the state of affairs by the euphemism at the head of this chapter. "They had a few words"—this is the immediate cause of many a domestic catastrophe. A young man was sent to Socrates to learn oratory. On being introduced to the philosopher he talked so incessantly that Socrates asked for double fees. "Why charge me double?" said the young fellow. "Because," said Socrates, "I must teach you two sciences; the one how to hold your tongue, and the other how to speak." It is impossible for people to be happy in matrimony who will not learn the first of these sciences.

We do not know whether Simonides was or was not a married man, but we fancy he must have been, for he used to say that he never regretted holding his tongue, but very often was sorry for having spoken. "Seest thou a man that is hasty in his words? There is more hope of a fool than of him." Sober second thoughts suggest palliatives and allowances that temper prevents us from noticing. The simple act of self-denial in restraining the expression of unpleasant feelings or harsh thoughts is the foundation stone of a happy home. For nothing draws people so closely together as the constant experience of mutual pleasure, and nothing so quickly drives them asunder as the frequent endurance of pain caused by one another's presence.

"One doth not know
How much an ill word may empoison liking."

Sometimes the husband blames the wife and the wife the husband when neither of them is at fault. This always reminds us of Pat's mistake. Two Irishmen walking along the same street, but coming from opposite directions, approached, both smiling and apparently recognizing one another. As they came closer they discovered that it was a mutual mistake. Equal to the occasion one of them said, "Och, my friend, I see how it is. You thought it was me, and I thought it was you, and now it's naythur of us."

Burton tells of a woman who, hearing one of her "gossips" complain of her husband's impatience, told her an excellent remedy for it. She gave her a glass of water, which, when he brawled, she should hold still in her mouth. She did so two or three times with great success, and at length, seeing her neighbour, she thanked her for it, and asked to know the ingredients. She told her that it was "fair water," and nothing more, for it was not the water, but her silence which performed the cure.

There are people who are kind in their actions and yet brutal in their speech, and they forget that it is not every one who can bear, like Boswell, to be told he is a fool. A woman may think she is always right and her husband always wrong, but it does not make the wheels of domestic life run smoother to say this in plain English. A man may have a contempt for his wife's dearest brother, but to tell the wife or brother so is not conducive to harmony.

It has sometimes been remarked that the marriage of a deaf and dumb man to a blind woman would have obvious advantages. Each of the parties would acquire an opportunity to practise little pantomimic scenes from which ordinary married folks are debarred. When they quarrelled, for instance—the wife being unable to see, while the husband could not hear or speak—she could hurl at him broadside after broadside of steel-pointed invective; and the poor man could but stand there, study the motion of her lips, and fondly imagine she was telling him how sorry she was that anything should come between them. He, on the other hand, could sit down, shake his fists, and make hideous grimaces, she all the while thinking he was sitting with his face buried in his hands, and hot remorseful tears streaming from his eyes. Husbands and wives who are not deprived of the use of their faculties might take the hint and resolve not to use them too keenly on certain occasions. In a matrimonial quarrel they need not hear or see everything.

"If you your lips would keep from slips,
Five things observe with care:
Of whom you speak, *to* whom you speak
And *how*, and *when*, and *where*.

The "last word" is the most dangerous of infernal machines. Husband and wife should no more fight to get it than they would struggle for the possession of a lighted bomb-shell. What is the use of the last word? After getting it a husband might perhaps, as an American newspaper suggests, advertise to whistle for a wager against a locomotive; but in every other respect his victory would be useless and painful. It would be a Cadmean victory in which the victor would suffer as much as the vanquished. A farmer cut down a tree which stood so near the boundary line of his farm that it was doubtful whether it belonged to him or to his neighbour. The neighbour, however, claimed the tree, and prosecuted the man who cut it for damages. The case was sent from court to court. Time was wasted and temper lost; but the case was finally gained by the prosecutor. The last of the transaction was that the man who gained the cause went to the lawyer's office to execute a deed of his whole farm, which he had been compelled to sell to pay his costs! Then, houseless and homeless, he thrust his hands into his pockets, and triumphantly exclaimed, "I've beat him!" In the same way husband and wife may become bankrupt of heart-wealth by endeavouring to get the last word.

Men sometimes become fractious from pure monotony. When they are unable to find subjects for profitable conversation there arises a propensity to "nag" and find fault. In a Russian story, the title of which in English is "Buried Alive," two prisoners are talking in the night, and one relates: "I had got, somehow or other, in the way of beating her (his wife). Some days I would keep at it from morning till night. I did not know what to do with myself when I was not beating her. She used to sit crying, and I could not help feeling sorry for her, and so I beat her." Subsequently he murdered her. Are there not men above the class of wife-beaters who indulge in fault-finding, "nagging," and other forms of tongue-castigation? They have got into the habit. They do not know what to do with themselves when not so employed. The tears of their wives only irritate them.

Of course some wives are quite capable of giving as much as they get. It is said that at a recent fashionable wedding, after the departure of the happy pair, a dear little girl, whose papa and mamma were among the guests, asked, with a child's innocent inquisitiveness: "Why do they throw things at the pretty lady in the carriage?" "For luck, dear," replied one of the bridesmaids. "And why," again asked the child, "doesn't she throw them back?" "Oh," said the young lady, "that would be rude." "No it wouldn't," persisted the dear little thing to the delight of her doting parents who stood by: "ma does."

"As the climbing up a sandy way is to the feet of the aged, so is a wife full of words to a quiet man." She who "has a tongue of her own" has always more last words to say, and, if she ever does close her mouth, the question suggests itself whether she should not be arrested for carrying concealed weapons. On the tombs of such wives might be inscribed epitaphs like the following, which is to be found in a churchyard in Surrey—

"Here lies, returned to clay,
Miss Arabella Young,
Who on the first of May
Began to hold her tongue."

Poor Caudle, as a rule, thought discretion the better part of valour, and sought refuge in the arms of soothing slumber; but there are some men who do not allow their wives to have it all their own way without at least an occasional protest. "Do you pretend to have as good a judgment as I have?" said an enraged wife to her husband. "Well, no," he replied, deliberately; "our choice of partners for life shows that my judgment is not to be compared to yours." When they have "a few words," however, the woman usually has the best of it. "See here," said a fault-finding husband, "we must have things arranged in this house so that we shall know where everything is kept." "With all my heart," sweetly answered his wife, "and let us begin with your late hours, my love. I should much like to know where they are kept."

Such matrimonial word-battles may amuse outsiders as the skill of gladiators used to amuse, but the combatants make themselves very miserable. Far better to be incapable of making a repartee if we only use the power to wound the feelings of the one whom we have vowed to love. There is an art of putting things that should be studied by married people. How many quarrels would be avoided if we could always say with courtesy and tact any unpleasant thing that may have to be said! It is related of a good-humoured celebrity that when a man once stood before him and his friend at the theatre, completely shutting out all view of the stage, instead of asking him to sit down, or in any way giving offence, he simply said, "I beg your pardon, sir; but when you see or hear anything particularly interesting on the stage, will you please let us know, as we are entirely dependent on your kindness?" That was sufficient. With a smile and an apology that only the art of putting things could have extracted, the gentleman took his seat. There is a story of a separation which took place simply because a gracious announcement had been couched by a husband in ungracious terms. "My dear, here is a little present I have brought to make you good-tempered." "Sir," was the indignant reply, "do you dare to say that it is necessary to bribe me into being good-tempered? Why, I am always good-tempered; it is your violent temper, sir!" And so the quarrel went on to the bitter end.

It is a very difficult thing to find fault well. We all have to find fault at times, in reference to servants, children, husband, or wife; but in a great number of cases the operation loses half its effect, or has no effect at all, perhaps a downright bad effect, because of the way in which it is done. Above all things remember this caution, never to find fault when out of temper. Again, there is a time *not* to find fault, and in the right perception of when that time is lies no small part of the art. The reproof which has most sympathy in it will be most effectual. It understands and allows for infirmity. It was this sympathy that prompted Dr. Arnold to take such pains in studying the characters of his pupils, so that he might best adapt correction to each particular case.

The very worst time for a husband and wife to have "a few words" is dinner-time, because, if we have a good dinner, our attention should be bestowed on what we are eating. He who bores us at dinner robs us of pleasure and injures our health, a fact which the alderman realized when he exclaimed to a stupid interrogator, "With your confounded questions, sir, you've made me swallow a piece of green fat without tasting it." Many a poor wife has to swallow her dinner without tasting it because her considerate husband chooses this time to find fault with herself, the children, the servants, and with everything except himself. The beef is too much done, the vegetables too little, everything is cold. "I think you might look after something! Oh! that is no excuse," and so on, to the great disturbance of his own and his wife's digestion. God sends food, but the devil sends the few cross words that prevent it from doing us any good. We should have at least three laughs during dinner, and every one is bound to contribute a share of agreeable table-talk, good-humour, and cheerfulness.

"In politics," said Cavour, "nothing is so absurd as rancour." In the same way we may say that nothing is so absurd in matrimony as sullen silence. Reynolds in his "Life and Times" tells of a free-and-easy actor who passed three festive days at the seat of the Marquis and Marchioness of —— without any invitation, convinced (as proved to be the case) that, my lord and my lady not being on *speaking terms*, each would suppose the other had asked him. A soft answer turns away wrath, and when a wife or a husband is irritated there is nothing like letting a subject drop. Then silence is indeed golden. But the silence persisted in—as by the lady in the old comedy, who, in reply to her husband's "For heaven's sake, my dear, do tell me what you mean," obstinately keeps her lips closed—is an instrument of deadly torture. "A wise man by his words maketh himself beloved." To this might be added that on certain occasions a fool by his obstinate silence maketh himself hated.

"According to Milton, 'Eve kept silence in Eden to hear her husband talk,'" said a gentleman to a lady friend; and then added, in a melancholy tone, "Alas! there have been no Eves since." "Because," quickly retorted the lady, "there have been no husbands worth listening to." Certainly there are too few men who exert themselves to be as agreeable to their wives (their best friends), as they are to the comparative strangers or secret enemies whom they meet at clubs and other places of resort. And yet if it is true that "to be agreeable in our family circle is not only a positive duty but an absolute morality," then every husband and wife should say on their wedding day—

"To balls and routs for fame let others roam,
Be mine the happier lot to please at home."

In one of the letters of Robertson, of Brighton, he tells of a lady who related to him "the delight, the tears of gratitude which she had witnessed in a poor girl to whom, in passing, I gave a kind look on going out of church on Sunday. What a lesson! How cheaply happiness can be given! What opportunities we miss of doing an angel's work! I remember doing it, full of sad feelings, passing on, and thinking no more about it; and it gave an hour's sunshine to a human life, and lightened the load of life to a human heart for a time!" If even a look can do so much, who shall estimate the power of kind or unkind words in making married life happy or miserable? In the home circle more than anywhere else—

"Words are mighty, words are living:
Serpents with their venomous stings,
Or bright angels, crowding round us,

With heaven's light upon their wings:
Every word has its own spirit,
True or false that never dies;
Every word man's lips have uttered
Echoes in God's skies."

CHAPTER XXIII.

PULLING TOGETHER.

"When souls, that should agree to will the same,
To have one common object for their wishes,
Look different ways, regardless of each other,
Think what a train of wretchedness ensues!"

Said a husband to his angry wife: "Look at Carlo and Kitty asleep on the rug; I wish men lived half as agreeably with their wives." "Stop!" said the lady. "Tie them together, and see how they will agree!" If men and women when tied together sometimes agree very badly what is the reason? Because instead of pulling together each of them wishes to have his or her own way. But when they do pull together what greater thing is there for them than "to feel that they are joined for life, to strengthen each other in all labour, to rest on each other in all sorrow, to minister to each other in all pain, to be one with each other in the silent unspeakable memories at the moment of the last parting?"

What is meant by pulling together may be explained by referring to the custom of the "Dunmow flitch," which was founded by Juga, a noble lady, in A.D. IIII, and restored by Robert de Fitzwalter, in 1244. It was that any person from any part of England going to Dunmow in Essex, and humbly kneeling on two stones at the church door, may claim a gammon of bacon if he can swear that for twelve months and a day he has never had a household brawl or wished himself unmarried. Hence the phrase "He may fetch a flitch of bacon from Dunmow," *i.e.*, He is so amiable and good-tempered that he will never quarrel with his wife. To eat Dunmow bacon is to live in conjugal amity. There were only eight claimants admitted to eat the flitch between the years 1244-1772, a number that seems to justify Prior's sarcastic couplet:

"Ah, madam, cease to be mistaken,
Few married fowl peck Dunmow bacon."

It is a great pity that "few married fowl peck Dunmow bacon," for those that do are so happy that they may be called birds of Paradise.

"A well-matched couple carry a joyful life between them, as the two spies carried the cluster of Eshcol. They multiply their joys by sharing them, and lessen their troubles by dividing them: this is fine arithmetic. The waggon of care rolls lightly along as they pull together, and when it drags a little heavily, or there's a hitch anywhere, they love each other all the more, and so lighten the labour." When there is wisdom in the husband there is generally gentleness in the wife, and between them the old wedding wish is worked out: "One year of joy, another of comfort, and all the rest of content."

When two persons without any spiritual affinity are bound together in irrevocable bondage, it is to their "unspeakable weariness and despair," and life becomes to them "a drooping and disconsolate household captivity, without refuge or redemption." Such unions are marriages only in name. They are a mere housing together.

However, this doctrine may easily be exaggerated, and certainly married people ought to be very slow in allowing themselves to think that it is impossible for them to hit it off or pull with the partners of their lives. Those who cherish unhealthy sentimentalism on this subject would do well to brace themselves up by reading a little of the robust common sense of Dr. Johnson. Talking one evening of Mrs. Careless, the doctor said: "If I had married her, it might have been as happy for me." *Boswell*: "Pray, sir, do you not suppose that there are fifty women in the world, with any one of whom a man may be as happy as with any one woman in particular?" *Johnson*: "Ay, sir, fifty thousand." *Boswell*: "Then, sir, you are not of opinion with some who imagine that certain men and certain women are made for each other; and that they cannot be happy if they miss their counterparts." *Johnson*: "To be sure not, sir. I believe marriages would in general be as happy, and often more so, if they were all made by the Lord Chancellor, upon a due consideration of the characters and circumstances, without the parties having any choice in the matter."

The following, too, is interesting, for we may gather from it how, in Johnson's opinion, the feat of living happily with any one of fifty thousand women could be accomplished. The question was started one evening whether people who differed on some essential point could live in friendship together. Johnson said they might. Goldsmith said they could not, as they had not the *idem velle atque idem nolle*—the same likings and the same aversions. *Johnson*: "Why, sir, you must shun the subject as to which you disagree. For instance, I can live very well with Burke; I love his knowledge, his genius, his diffusion, and affluence of conversation; but I would not talk to him of the Rockingham party." *Goldsmith*: "But, sir, when people live together who have something as to which they disagree, and which they want to shun, they will be in the situation mentioned in the story of Bluebeard, 'You may look into all the chambers but one.' But we should have the greatest inclination to look into that chamber, to talk over that subject." *Johnson* (with a loud voice): "Sir, I am not saying that *you* could live in friendship with a man from whom you differ as to some point: I am only saying that *I* could do it."

In matrimony, as in religion, in things essential there should be unity, in things indifferent diversity, in all things charity.

In matrimony, though it is the closest and dearest friendship, shades of character and the various qualities of mind and heart, never approximate to such a degree, as to preclude all possibility of misunderstanding. But the broad and firm principles upon which all honourable and enduring sympathy is founded, the love of truth, the reverence for right, the abhorrence of all that is base and unworthy, admit of no difference or misunderstanding; and where these exist in the relations of two people united for life, love, and happiness, as perfect as this imperfect existence affords, may be realized. But the rule is different in matters that are not essential. In reference to these married people should cultivate "the sympathy of difference." They should agree to differ each respecting the tastes and prejudices of the other.

At no time are husbands and wives seen to greater advantage than when yielding their own will in unimportant matters to the will of another, and we quite agree with a writer who makes the following remark: "Great actions are so often performed from little motives of vanity, self-complacency, and the like, that I am apt to think more highly of the person whom I observe checking a reply to a petulant speech, or even submitting to the judgment of another *in stirring the fire*, than of one who gives away thousands!"

In all things there should be charity. Dolly Winthrop in "Silas Marner" was patiently tolerant of her husband, "considering that men would be so," and viewing the stronger sex "in the light of animals whom it pleased Heaven to make troublesome like bulls or turkey cocks." This sensible woman knew that if at times her husband was troublesome he had his good qualities. On these she would accustom herself to dwell.

A Scotch minister, being one day engaged in visiting his flock, came to the door of a house where his gentle tapping could not be heard for the noise of contention within. After waiting a little he opened the door and walked in, saying, with an authoritative voice: "I should like to know who is the head of this house?" "Weel, sir," said the husband and father, "if ye sit doon a wee, we'll maybe be able to tell ye, for we're just tryin' to settle the point." Merely to settle this point some married people are continually engaging in a tug of war instead of pulling comfortably together. But what a mean contest! How much better it would be only to strive who should love the other most! To married people especially are these words of Marcus Aurelius applicable: "We are made for co-operation, like feet, like hands, like eyelids, like the rows of the upper and lower teeth. To act against one another, then, is contrary to nature."

That union is strength is forcibly, if not very elegantly, illustrated by Erskine's description of a lodging where he had passed the night. He said that the fleas were so numerous and so ferocious that if they had been but *unanimous* they would have pulled him out of bed. If husband and wife would be but unanimous they would be a match against every enemy to their felicity. On the other hand, how impossible it is for those who work against each other to live together with any advantage or comfort. We all remember the illustration of Æsop. A charcoal-burner carried on his trade in his own house. One day he met a friend, a fuller, and entreated him to come and live with him, saying that they should be far better neighbours, and that their housekeeping expenses would be lessened. The fuller replied, "The arrangement is impossible as far as I am concerned, for whatever I should whiten, you would immediately blacken again with your charcoal."

One secret of pulling together is not to interfere with what does not concern us. A man who can trust his wife should no more meddle with her home concerns than she should pester him with questions about his business. He will never be able to pull with her if he pokes over the weekly bills, insists on knowing how much each thing is per pound, and what he is going to have every day for dinner. It is indeed almost a *sine quâ non* of domestic felicity that *paterfamilias* should be absent from home at least six hours in the day. Jones asked his wife, "Why is a husband like dough?" He expected she would give it up, and he was going to tell her that it was because a woman needs him; but she said it was because he was hard to get off her hands.

Of course, like every other good rule, this one of non-intervention may be carried too far, as it was by the studious man who said, when a servant told him that his house was on fire, "Go to your mistress, you know I have no charge of household matters." No doubt occasions will arise when a husband will be only too glad to take counsel with his wife in business cares; while she may have to remember all her life long, with gratitude and love, some season of sickness or affliction, when he filled his own place and hers too, ashamed of no womanish task, and neither irritated nor humiliated by ever such trivial household cares.

"Parents and children seldom act in concert, each child endeavours to appropriate the esteem or fondness of the parents, and the parents, with yet less temptation, betray each other to their children; thus some place their confidence in the father, and some in the mother, and by degrees the house is filled with artifices and feuds." These words point to a danger to be guarded against by married people who desire to pull together. It is sad when a child is not loved equally by both its parents. In this case, however innocent and blessed the little one may be, it is liable to become the disturber of parental peace.

Perhaps the way Carlyle and his wife pulled together is not so very uncommon. His mother used to say of him that he was "gey ill to live with," and Miss Welsh whom he married had a fiery temper. When provoked she "was as hard as a flint, with possibilities of dangerous sparks of fire." The pair seem to have tormented each other, but not half as much as each tormented him and herself. They were too like each other, suffering in the same way from nerves disordered, digestion impaired, excessive self-consciousness, and the absence of children to take their thoughts away from each other. They were, in the fullest sense of the word, everything to each other—both for good and evil, sole comforters, chief tormentors. The proverb "Ill to hae but waur to want" was true of the Carlyles as of many another couple.

Sir David Baird and some other English officers, being captured by Tippo Saib, were confined for some time in one of the dungeons of his palace at Bangalore. When Sir David's mother heard the news in Scotland, referring to the method in which prisoners were chained together and to her son's well-known irascible temper, she exclaimed: "God pity the lad that's tied to our Davie." How much more to be pitied is he or she whom matrimony has tied for life to a person with a bad temper!

Over-particularity in trifles causes a great deal of domestic discomfort. The husband or wife who, to use a common phrase, wishes a thing to be "just so," and not otherwise, is uncomfortable to pull with. For any person to be thoroughly amiable and livable with, there should be a little touch of untidiness and unpreciseness, and indifference to small things. A little spice—not too much—of the Irishman's spirit who said, "If you can't take things asy, take them as asy as you can."

There is no more beautiful quality than that ideality which conceives and longs after perfection; but if too exclusively cultivated it may drag down rather than elevate its possessor. The faculty which is ever conceiving and desiring something better and more perfect must be modified in its action by good sense, patience, and conscience, otherwise it induces a morbid, discontented spirit, which courses through the veins of individual and family life like a subtle poison.

Exactingsness is untrained ideality, and much domestic misery is caused by it. A little bit of conscience makes the exacting person sour. He fusses, fumes, finds fault, and scolds because everything is not perfect in an imperfect world. Much more happy and good is he whose conceptions and desire of excellence are equally strong, but in whom there is a greater amount of discriminating common-sense.

Most people can see what is faulty in themselves and their surroundings; but while the dreamer frets and wears himself out over the unattainable, the happy, practical man is satisfied with what *can* be attained. There was much wisdom in the answer given by the principal of a large public institution when complimented on his habitual cheerfulness amid a diversity of cares: "I've made up my mind," he said, "to be satisfied when things are done *half* as well as I would have them."

Ideality often becomes an insidious mental and moral disease, acting all the more subtlely from its alliance with what is noblest in us.

The virtue of conscientiousness may turn into the vice of censoriousness if misapplied. It was the constant prayer of the great and good Bishop Butler that he might be saved from what he called "scrupulosity." Dr. Johnson used to admire this wise sentence in Thomas à Kempis: "Be not angry that you cannot make others as you wish them to be, since you cannot make yourself as you wish to be." Searching for domestic happiness would not be as unsuccessful as it is with some people if they were not continually finding fault.

Jeremy Taylor impresses this fact by one of his quaint illustrations: "The stags in the Greek epigram, whose knees were clogged with frozen snow upon the mountains, came down to the brooks of the valleys, hoping to thaw their joints with the waters of the stream; but there the frost overtook them, and bound them fast in ice, till the young herdsmen took them in their stranger snare. It is the unhappy chance of many men finding many inconveniences upon the mountains of single life, they descend into the valleys of marriage to refresh their troubles, and there they enter into fetters, and are bound to sorrow by the cords of a man's or woman's peevishness."

The Psalmist says that "God maketh men to be of one mind in a house." Let husband and wife live near Him, and He will enable them to avoid domestic strife which Cowper declares to be the "sorest ill of human life."

CHAPTER XXIV.

NETS AND CAGES.

"I think for a woman to fail to make and keep a happy home, is to be a 'failure' in a truer sense than to have failed to catch a husband."—*Frances Power Cobbe.*

"We think caged birds sing, when indeed they cry."—*Vittoria Corombona.*

When Mr. Wilberforce was a candidate for Hull, his sister, an amiable and witty young lady, offered a new dress to each of the wives of those freemen who voted for her brother. When saluted with "Miss Wilberforce for ever!" she pleasantly observed, "I thank you, gentlemen, but I cannot agree with you, for really I do not wish to be *Miss* Wilberforce for ever."

We do not blame Miss Wilberforce or any other young lady for not wishing to be a "Miss" for ever; but we desire to point out in this chapter that all is not done when the husband is gained.

"Even in the happiest choice whom fav'ring Heaven
Has equal love and easy fortune given;
Think not, the husband gained, that all is done,
The prize of happiness must still be won;
And oft the careless find it to their cost;
The lover in the husband may be lost;

The graces might alone his heart allure;
They and the virtues meeting must secure."

According to Dean Swift, "the reason why so few marriages are happy is because young women spend their time in making nets, not in making cages." Certainly a bird in the hand is worth two in the bush, and girls are quite justified in trying in all ways, consistent with modesty and self-respect, to net husbands. Still, she is the really fine woman who can not merely net the affections of a husband during the honeymoon, but who can cage and keep them throughout a long married life. Only the other day, a man told me that after forty years of married life, he loved his wife almost better than the day they were married. We are not told that Alexander the Great, after conquering the world, kept his conquest very long, but this wife kept her conquest forty years. Woman in her time has been called upon to endure a great deal of definition. She had been described as, "A good idea—spoiled!" This may be true of one who can only make nets, but it certainly is not true of a cage-maker. Always do—

"Her air, her smile, her motions, tell
Of womanly completeness;
A music as of household songs
Is in her voice of sweetness.

Flowers spring to blossom where she walks
The careful ways of duty;
The hard stiff lines of life with her
Are flowing curves of beauty."

Men are often as easily caught as birds, but as difficult to keep. If the wife cannot make her home bright and happy, so that it shall be the cleanest, sweetest, cheerfullest place that her husband can find refuge in—a retreat from the toils and troubles of the outer world—then God help the poor man, for he is virtually homeless!

In the home more than anywhere else order is Heaven's first law. It is the duty of a wife to sweetly order her cage so that it may be clean, neat, and free from muddle. Method is the oil that makes the wheels of the domestic machine run easily. The mistress of a home who desires order, and the tranquillity that comes of order, must insist on the application of method to every branch and department of the household work. She must rise and breakfast early and give her orders early. Doing much before twelve o'clock gives her a command of the day.

A friend of Robert Hall, the famous preacher, once asked him regarding a lady of their acquaintance, "Will she make a good wife for me?" "Well," replied Hall, "I can hardly say—I never lived with her!" This is the real test of happiness in married life. It is one thing to see ladies on "dress" occasions and when every effort is being made to please them; it is quite another thing to see them amidst the varied and often conflicting circumstances of household life. Men may talk in raptures of youth and beauty, wit and sprightliness; but after seven years of union, not one of them is to be compared to good family management which is seen at every meal, and felt every hour in the husband's purse. In the "Records of Later Life," Fanny Kemble (Mrs. Butler), shortly after she had begun housekeeping with a staff of six servants, writes from America to a friend, "I have been reproaching myself, and reproving others, and heartily regretting that instead of Italian and music, I had not learned a little domestic economy, and how much bread, butter, flour, eggs, milk, sugar, and meat ought to be consumed per week by a family of eight persons." There is no reason why she should not have learned all this, and Italian and music as well.

Gradually it has come to be seen that practical cookery, which might be classed under the head of chemistry, is an excellent intellectual training, as it teaches the application in daily life of knowledge derived from a variety of branches of study. From this point of view even sweet girl-graduates may take pride in being good cooks, while as regards women of the working classes hardly anything drives their husbands to drink so much as bad cookery and irregular meals.

Leigh Hunt used to say that "the most fascinating women are those that can most enrich the every-day moments of existence." If we are to believe Mrs. Carlyle, who lived next door to the Hunts at Chelsea, Mrs. Hunt did not do much in the way of domestic economy to "enrich the every-day moments of existence." "I told Mrs. Hunt, one day, I had been very busy *painting*." "What?" she asked, "is it a portrait?" "Oh! no," I told her; "something of more importance—a large wardrobe." She could not imagine, she said, "how I could have patience for such things." And so, having no patience for them herself, what is the result? She is every other day reduced to borrow my tumblers, my tea-cups; even a cupful of porridge, a few spoonfuls of tea, are begged of me, because "Missus has got company, and happens to be out of the article;' in plain anadorned English, because 'missus' is the most wretched of managers, and is often at the point of having not a copper in her purse. To see how they live and waste here, it is a wonder the whole city does not 'bankrape, and go out o' sicht';—flinging platefuls of what they are pleased to denominate 'crusts' (that is, what I consider all the best of the bread) into the ashpits.' I often say, with honest self-congratulation, 'In Scotland we have no such thing as "crusts."' On the whole, though the English ladies seem to have their wits more at their finger-ends, and have a great advantage over me in that respect, I never cease to be glad that I was born on the other side of the Tweed, and that those who are nearest and dearest to me are Scotch.... Mrs. Hunt I shall soon be quite terminated with, I foresee. She torments my life out with borrowing. She actually borrowed one of the brass fenders the other day, and I had difficulty in getting it out of her hands; irons, glasses, tea-cups, silver spoons are in constant requisition; and when one sends for them the whole number can never be found. Is it not a shame to manage so, with eight guineas a week to keep house on! It makes me very indignant to see all the waste that goes on around me, when I am needing so much care and calculation to make ends meet."

When Carlyle was working hard to support himself and his wife by literature at the lonely farmhouse which was their home, Mrs. Carlyle did all she could to mitigate by good cookery the miseries which dyspepsia inflicted upon him. She thus writes of her culinary trials: "The bread, above all, brought from Dumfries, 'soured on his stomach' (Oh Heaven!), and it was plainly my duty as a Christian wife to bake at home; so I sent for Cobbett's 'Cottage Economy,' and fell to work at a loaf of bread. But knowing nothing about the process of fermentation or the heat of ovens, it came to pass that my loaf got put into the oven at the time that myself ought to have been put into bed; and I remained the only person not asleep in a house in the middle of a desert. One o'clock struck, and then two, and then three; and still I was sitting there in an immense solitude, my whole body aching with weariness, my heart aching with a sense of forlornness and degradation. That I, who had been so petted at home, whose comfort had been studied by everybody in the house, who had never been required to do anything but cultivate my mind, should have to pass all those hours of the night in watching a loaf of bread—which mightn't turn out bread after all! Such thoughts maddened me, till I laid down my head on the table and sobbed aloud. It was then that somehow the idea of Benvenuto Cellini sitting up all night watching his Perseus in the furnace came into my head, and suddenly I asked myself: 'After all, in the sight of the Upper Powers, what is the mighty difference between a statue of Perseus and a loaf of bread, so that each be the thing one's hand has found to do? The man's determined will, his energy, his patience, his resource, were the really admirable things of which his statue of Perseus was the mere chance expression. If he had been a woman living at Craigenputtoch, with a dyspeptic husband, sixteen miles from a baker, and he a bad one, all these same qualities would have come out more fitly in a good loaf of bread.' I cannot express what consolation this germ of an idea spread over my uncongenial life during the years we lived at that savage place, where my two immediate predecessors had gone mad, and the third had taken to drink."

Though the life of that tragic muse Mrs. Siddons was girded about with observance and worship from the highest in the land, though her mind and imagination were always employed in realizing the most glorious creations of the most glorious poets, Mrs. Siddons in her home was at once the simplest and the tenderest of women. She did a great deal of the household work herself, and her grand friends, when they called, would be met by her with a flat-iron in her hand, or would find her seated studying a new part, while, at the same time, she rocked the cradle of her latest born, and knitted her husband's stockings. When she went to the theatre she was generally accompanied by one or more of her children, and the little things would cling about her, holding her hand or her dress, as she stood in the side scenes. The fine ladies who petted her could not put one grain of their fine-ladyism into her. To the end of her life she remained a proof of the not-generally-believed fact that an artist can be, at the same time, a most purely domestic woman. The same too may be said of a mathematician, for the greatest woman-mathematician of any age, Mary Somerville, was renowned for her good housekeeping.

An American newspaper lately addressed the following wise words to young women: "Learn to keep house. If you would be a level-headed woman; if you would have right instincts and profound views, and that most subtle, graceful, and irresistible of all things, womanly charm; if you would make your pen, your music, your accomplishments tell, and would give them body, character, and life; if you would be a woman of genuine power, and queen o'er all the earth, learn to keep house thoroughly and practically. You see the world all awry, and are consumed with a desire to set it right. Must you go on a mission to the heathen? Very well, but learn to keep house first. Begin reform, where all true reform must begin, at the centre and work outwards; at the foundation and work upwards. What is the basis and centre of all earthly life? It is the family, the home; these relations dictate and control all others. *There is nothing from which this distracted world is suffering so much to-day, as for want of thorough housekeeping and homemaking.*"

But a cage-making wife is much more than a good cook and housekeeper. Indeed it is possible for a wife to be too careful and cumbered about these things. When such is the case she becomes miserable and grumbles at a little dust or disorder which the ordinary mortal does not see, just as a fine musician is pained and made miserable at a slight discord that is not noticed by less-trained ears. Probably her husband wishes his house were less perfectly kept, but more peaceful. A woman should know when to change her *rôle* of housewife for that of the loving friend and companion of her husband. She should be able and willing to intelligently discuss with him the particular political or social problem that is to him of vital interest. We will all agree with Dr. Johnson that a man of sense and education should seek a suitable *companion* in a wife. "It was," he said, "a miserable thing when the conversation could only be such as, whether the mutton should be boiled or roast, and probably a dispute about that." A good and loyal wife takes upon her a share of everything that concerns and interests her husband. Whatever may be his work or even recreation, she endeavours to learn enough about it to be able to listen to him with interest if he speaks to her of it, and to give him a sensible opinion if he asks for it. In every matter she is helpful.

Women's lives are often very dull; but it would help to make them otherwise if wives would sometimes think over, during the hours when parted from their husbands, a few little winning ways as surprises for them on their return, either in the way of conversation, or of some small change of dress, or any way their ingenuity would have suggested in courting days. How little the lives of men and women would be dull, if they thought of and acted towards each other after marriage as they did before it!

Certainly, it does a wife good to go out of her cage occasionally for amusement, although her deepest, truest happiness may be found at home. She, quite as much as her husband, requires change and recreation, but while this is true she must never forget that a life of pleasure is a life of pain, and that if much of her time is spent in visiting and company, anarchy and confusion at home must be the consequence. "Never seek for amusement," says Mr. Ruskin, "but be always ready to be amused. The least thing has play in it—the slightest word wit, when your hands are busy and your heart is free. But if you make the aim of your life amusement, the day will come when all the agonies of a pantomime will not bring you an honest laugh."

Nothing renders a woman so agreeable to her husband as good humour. It possesses the powers ascribed to magic and imparts beauty to the plainest features. On the other hand, the bright, sparkling girl, who turns, after marriage, in her hours of privacy with her husband, into the dull, silent, or grumbling wife has no one to thank but herself if he is often absent from his home.

Men hate nagging, and, indeed, husband-nagging is almost as cruel as wife-beating. There are women whose perpetual contentiousness is a moral reproduction of an Oriental torture, that drops water on you every ten seconds. The butler of a certain Scottish laird, who had been in the family a number of years, at last resigned his situation because his lordship's wife was always scolding him. "Oh!" exclaimed his master, "if that be all, ye've very little to complain of." "Perhaps so," replied the butler; "but I have decided in my own mind to put up with it no longer." "Go, then," said his lordship; "and be thankful for the rest of your life that ye're not married to her."

The methods which women adopt in managing husbands vary with the characters of the individuals to be guided. In illustration of this here is a short story. Two women, Mrs. A. and Mrs. B., were talking together one day with some friends over a cup of tea, when the subject of the management of husbands came up. Each of these two wives boasted that she could make her husband do exactly what she liked. A spinster who was present, Miss C, denied the truth of this statement, and this led to high words, in the course of which it was agreed that each wife should prove her power by making her husband drive her on a particular afternoon in a hired carriage to an appointed place, which we will call Edmonton. The test was considered a good one, because the two husbands were individuals inclined to economy, who in the ordinary course of events would never think of hiring a carriage or driving anywhere, excepting in a 'bus to the City. Mrs. A. was a strong-minded, determined woman, and Mr. A. was meek and gentle; no one doubted, therefore, that Mrs. A. could get what she wanted. But Mr. B. was an argumentative, contradictory, wilful, and pugnacious individual, while Mrs. B. was sweet and good. It was expected that Mrs. B. would have to own herself defeated. However, the day arrived and the hour, the unbelieving spinster repaired to the spot, and up drove the two husbands with their wives sitting in state by their sides. "How did you manage it?" said Miss C. "Oh," said Mrs. A., "I simply said to my husband, 'Mr. A., I wish you to hire a carriage and drive me to Edmonton.' He said, 'Very well, my dear, but I——,' and here I am." "And how did you manage it, Mrs. B.?" Mrs. B. was unwilling to confess, but at length she was induced to do so. "I said to my husband, 'I think Mr. and Mrs. A. are very extravagant: they are going to hire a carriage and pair to-morrow and drive to Edmonton.' 'Why should they not do so if they like it?' said Mr. B. 'Oh, no reason at all, my dear, if you think it right, and if they can afford it; but we could not do anything of that kind, of course. Besides, I fancy Mr. A. is more accustomed to driving than you are.' 'A. is not at all more accustomed to it than I am,' said Mr. B., 'and I can afford it quite as well as he. Indeed, I will prove that I can and will, for I will hire a carriage and drive there at the same time.' 'Very well, my dear, if you think so; but I should not like to go with you, I should feel so ashamed.' 'Then I wish you to go with me, Mrs. B.; I insist upon your accompanying me.' So," said quiet little Mrs. B., "that is the way I manage Mr. B."

Neither of these women is to be congratulated on her method of management. Each despised her husband, and what sort of basis is scorn for happiness in married life? If a man's own wife does not believe in him, and look up to him, and admire him, and like him better than anyone else, poor man, who else will? If he is not king at home, where is he king?

Once upon a time, according to an old heathen legend, the gods and goddesses were assembled together, and were talking over matters celestial, when one of the company, who was of an inquiring mind, said, "What are the people who live on the earth like?" No one knew. One or two guesses were made, but every one knew that they were only guesses. At last an enterprising little goddess suggested that a special messenger should be sent to visit the earth, to make inquiries, and to bring back information concerning the inhabitants thereof. Off the messenger went. On his return, the gods and goddesses once more assembled, and every one was very anxious to hear the result of this mission. "Well," said Jove, who constituted himself speaker on the occasion, "what have you learnt? What are the people of the earth like?" "They are very curious people," said the traveller. "They have no character of their own, but they become what others think them. If you think them cruel, they act cruelly; if you think them true, they may be relied on; if you think them false, they lie and steal; if you believe them to be kind, they are amiability itself."

May not the secret of how to manage a husband be found in this small fable? A woman has power over her husband (that is, legitimate and reasonable power, not power to make him hire a carriage, but power to make him kind, true, and persevering) in proportion to her belief in him. She is never so helpless with regard to him as when she has lost faith in him herself.

Milton tells us that a good wife is "heaven's last, best gift to man;" but what constitutes a good wife? Purity of thought and feeling, a generous cheerful temper, a disposition ready to forgive, patience, a high sense of duty, a cultivated mind, and a natural grace of manner. She should be able to govern her household with gentle resolution, and to take an intelligent interest in her husband's pursuits. She should have a clear understanding, and "all the firmness that does not exclude delicacy," and "all the softness that does not imply weakness." "Her beauty, like the rose it resembleth, shall retain its sweetness when its bloom is withered. Her hand seeketh employment; her foot delighteth not in gadding about. She is clothed with neatness; she is fed with temperance. On her tongue dwelleth music; the sweetness of honey floweth from her lips. Her eye speaketh softness and love; but discretion, with a sceptre, sitteth on her brow. She presideth in the house, and there is peace; she commandeth with judgment, and is obeyed. She ariseth in the morning, she considers her affairs, and appointeth to every one their proper business. The prudence of her management is an honour to her husband; and he heareth her praise with a secret delight. Happy is the man that hath made her his wife; happy is the child that calleth her mother."

The married man must have been blessed with a cage-making wife like this who defined woman as "An essay on goodness and grace, in one volume, elegantly bound." Although it may seem a little expensive, every man should have a copy.

CHAPTER XXV.

HUSBANDS HAVE DUTIES TOO.

"A good wife is the gift of a good God, and the workmanship of a good husband."—*Proverb.*

"My dear sir, mind your studies, mind your business, *make your lady happy*, and be a good Christian."—*Dr. Johnson's advice to Boswell.*

A highland horse dealer, who lately effected a sale, was offered a bottle of porter to confess the animal's failings. The bottle was drunk, and he then said the horse had but two faults. When turned loose in the field he was "bad to catch," and he was "of no use when caught." Many a poor woman might say the same of her husband. She had to make many nets, for he was "bad to catch," and when caught—well, he forgot that husbands have duties as well as wives. Some men can neither do without wives nor with them; they are wretched alone, in what is called single blessedness, and they make their homes miserable when they get married; they are like the dog, which could not bear to be loose, and howled when it was tied up.

There are men with whom all the pleasure of love exists in its pursuit, and not in its possession. When a woman marries one of this class, he seems almost to despise her from that day. Having got her into his power he begins to bully her.

If it be true that there are more people married than keep good houses, husbands are quite as much to blame as wives. The proverb tells us that good wives and good plantations are made by good husbands. In the last chapter we ventured to suggest that women should make cages as well as nets; but all their efforts will be in vain if they have ill-birds who foul their own nests. To complete the subject, therefore, something must be said about the behaviour of the male bird when caught and caged.

First of all he should sing and not cry. How many women are there who suffer from the want of a kindly love, a sweet appreciation of their goodness and their self-sacrifice! How often will wives do tender and loving offices, adorn the home with flowers, making it as neat as the nest of a bird; dress their persons with elegance, and their faces with smiles, and find as a reward for this the stolid indifference of the block or the stupid insensibility of the lower animal! "She was a woman," wrote one who knew her sex well; "a woman down to the very tips of her finger-nails, and what she wanted was praise from the lips that she loved. Do you ask what that meant? Did she want gold, or dress, or power? No; all she wanted was that which will buy us all, and which so few of us ever get—in a word, it was Love."

Priscilla Lammeter, in "Silas Marner," well understood the selfish way many husbands fall into of relieving their feelings: "There's nothing kills a man so soon as having nobody to find fault with but himself. It's a deal the best way o' being master to let somebody else do the ordering, and keep the blaming in your own hands. It 'ud save many a man a stroke I believe."

"If he would only be satisfied!" Mrs. Carlyle used sometimes to complain of Carlyle, "but I have had to learn that when he does not find fault he is pleased, and that has to content me." On one occasion when Carlyle was away from home Mrs. Carlyle described her charwoman sort of work to get all in perfect order for her husband's arrival; and when all was complete—his dinner ready, his arm-chair in its usual attitude, his pipe and tobacco prepared, all looking as comfortable as possible—Mrs. C. sat down at last to rest, and to expect him with a quiet mind. He arrived; and "after he had just greeted me, what do you think he did? He walked to the window and shook it, and asked 'Where's the wedge of the window?' and until we had found that blessed wedge nothing would content him. He said the window would rattle and spoil all." When a great and good man gives such inordinate prominence to trivial worries, how intolerable to live with must be the baser sort, who scarcely know the meaning of self-control!

Some men may deserve rewards for distinguished service in action; but they certainly do not for distinguished service in passion or suffering. In this respect they are far less brave than women.

The fault of many husbands is not the absence of love, but their failure to express it in their daily lives, and the self-absorption which prevents them from knowing that their wives want something more than they give them. They do not pay that attention to little things on which so much of a woman's happiness depends.

"Instead of love being the occasion of all the misery of this world (as is sung by fantastic bards), the misery of this world is occasioned by there not being love enough." Certain it is, that as time goes on married life is not usually found to want less love, but more; not less expression of love, but more. Caroline Perthes, writing to her husband, is not content he should love her, but wishes the phlegmatic German would sometimes tell her so.

Husbands would be more considerate and less exacting if they realized the fact that a wife's work is never done. I have heard more than one lady remark that the greatest pleasure of hotel life, and of a visit to one's friends, is to be able to sit down to dinner without a knowledge of what is coming in the various courses.

The wife whose sympathy is always ready for her husband's out-of-door difficulties naturally expects that he should at least try to understand her housekeeping troubles. How many they are is known to every one who has "run" a house for even a short time. A woman may have much theoretical knowledge, but this will not prevent unlooked-for obstacles from arising. Annoyances caused by human frailty and the working of natural agents beset every practical housekeeper.

It is the unexpected that constantly happens, and the daily girding up to meet the emergencies of the hour is the task of every wife who seeks to make her home a comfortable, habitable abode. It is work—real, earnest work, quite as hard in its way as the husband's.

Husbands should know the value and the difficulty of the work of their wives, and should never forget that a little help is worth a great deal of fault-finding.

The husband's affection must never be merged in an overweening conceit of his authority. His rule must be the rule of reason and kindness, not of severity and caprice. He is the houseband and should bind all together like a corner-stone, but not crush everything like a mill-stone. Jeremy Taylor says: "The dominion of a man over his wife is no other than as the soul rules the body; for which it takes mighty care, and uses it with a delicate tenderness, and cares for it in all contingencies, and watches to keep it from all evils, and studies to make for it fair provisions, and very often is led by its inclinations and desires, and does never contradict its appetites but when they are evil, and then also not without some trouble and sorrow; and its government comes only to this, it furnishes the body with light and understanding; and the body furnishes the soul with hands and feet; the soul governs, because the body cannot else be happy; but the *government* is no other than *provision*, as a nurse governs a child, when she causes him to eat, and to be warm, and dry, and quiet."

It sometimes happens that she who ought to have most influence on her husband's mind has least. A man will frequently take the advice of a stranger who cares not for him, in preference to the cordial and sensible opinion of his own wife. Consideration of the domestic evils such a line of conduct is calculated to produce ought to prevent its adoption. Besides, there is in woman an intuitive quickness, a penetration, and a foresight, that make her advice very valuable. "If I was making up a plan of consequence," said Lord Bolingbroke, "I should like first to consult with a sensible woman." Many a man has been ruined by professed friends, because when his wife, with a woman's quick detection of character, saw through them and urged him to give them up, he would not do so. And if a wife is the partner of her husband's cares surely she ought also to be the companion of his pleasures. There are selfish husbands who go about amusing themselves; but in reference to their wives they seem to be of the same opinion as the ancient philosopher, who only approved of women leaving home three times in their lives—to be baptized, married, and buried! Does it never occur to such Egyptian taskmasters that all work and no play is quite as bad for women as for men, and that the wife who makes her cage comfortable should occasionally be offered and even urged to take a little amusement? I know of one wife who struck under such treatment. Whenever her husband spent his money and time too freely away from home, she used to take her child and go for a little excursion, which of course cost money. If he gave more "drinks" than he could afford to himself and to his club-companions, she used to frighten him into good behaviour by ordering a bottle of champagne for herself. Giving in this way a Roland for every Oliver, this really good wife soon brought her husband to see that his selfishness was a losing game.

Cobbett protests against a husband getting to like his club, or indeed any house, better than his own. When absent from necessity, there is no wound given to the heart of the wife; she concludes that her husband would be with her if he could, and that satisfies. Yet in these cases her feelings ought to be consulted as much as possible; she ought to be apprised of the probable duration of the absence, and of the time of return.

And what Cobbett preached upon this text he himself practised. He and a friend called Finnerty were dining with a mutual friend. At eleven o'clock Cobbett said to the host, "We must go; my wife will be frightened." "You do not mean to go home to-night," was the reply. "I told him I did; and then sent my son, who was with us, to order out the post-chaise. We had twenty-three miles to go, during which we debated the question whether Mrs. Cobbett would be up to receive us, I contending for the affirmative and he for the negative. She was up, and had a nice fire for us to sit down at. She had not committed the matter to a servant; her servants and children were all in bed; and she was up, to perform the duty of receiving her husband and his friend. 'You did not expect him?' said Finnerty. 'To be sure I did,' said she; 'he never disappointed me in his life.'"

We ourselves heard a wife saying to her husband only the other day, "I would rather you had done that than given me ten pounds." What had he done? Only put himself out a little to return home at the exact hour he had appointed to be with her. That the little attention gratified her so much will not seem strange to any one who has observed the power of little things in imparting either pleasure or pain.

A kind husband, when he goes from home, generally brings back some little present to his wife. Attentions like this keep fresh that element of romance which should never be entirely absent from married life. They remind the now staid, but still impressible matron, of the days of her maiden power, when a cold look from her brought winter into the room, and when the faintest wish would have sent a certain young gentleman on a walk of a dozen miles for the first violets. Yes, now and then give your wife a present—a real present, which, without involving undue expense, is good enough to compel a certain sacrifice, and suitable enough to make her cheek flush with delight at seeing that just as the bride was dearer than the sweetheart, the wife is yet dearer than the bride. There is quite as much human nature in a wife as in a husband (men forget this), and a little tender petting does her a great deal of good, and may even be better than presents.

What a model husband and father Macaulay would have been if he had married! His sister, Lady Trevelyan, says, that "those who did not know him at home, never knew him in his most brilliant, witty, and fertile vein." He was life and sunshine to young and old in the sombre house in Great Ormond Street, where the forlorn old father, like a blighted oak, lingered on in leafless decay, reading one long sermon to his family on Sunday afternoons, and another long sermon on Sunday evenings—"where Sunday walking for walking's sake was never allowed, and even going to a distant church was discouraged." Through this Puritanic gloom Macaulay shot like a sunbeam, and turned it into a fairy scene of innocent laughter and mirth. Against Macaulay, the author, severe things may be said; but as to his conduct in his own home—as a son, as a brother, and an uncle—it is only the barest justice to say that he appears to have touched the furthest verge of human virtue, sweetness, and generosity. His thinking was often, if not generally, pitched in what we must call a low key, but his action might put the very saints to shame. He reversed a practice too common among men of genius, who are often careful to display all their shining and attractive qualities to the outside world, and keep for home consumption their meanness, selfishness, and ill-temper. Macaulay struck no heroic attitude of benevolence, magnanimity, and aspiration before the world—rather the opposite; but in the circle of his home affections he practised those virtues without letting his right hand know what was done by his left.

Writing to his oldest and dearest friend in the first days of her overwhelming grief, Her Majesty the Queen described the Prince Consort as having been to her "husband, father, lover, master, friend, adviser, and guide." There could scarcely be a better description of what a husband ought to be.

CHAPTER XXVI.

THE HEALTH OF THE FAMILY.

"Reason's whole pleasure, all the joys of sense,
Lie in three words—health, peace, and competence.
But Health consists with temperance alone,
And Peace, O Virtue, peace is all thy own."—*Pope.*

"Better to hunt in fields for health unbought,
Than fee the doctor for a nauseous draught."—*Dryden.*

An eminent physician gave four rules for the preservation of health. When he died, his books were sold; one, which was said to contain very valuable precepts of health, but which the bidders were not permitted to open, sold at a high price. When the purchaser got it home he hastily proceeded to examine it, and was much disappointed at finding that it contained nothing more than four simple rules. He thought he had thrown his money away. But on further consideration he was induced to put the rules in practice; by doing so he was restored to a state of health to which he had long been a stranger. He often spoke of the old physician's book as the cheapest and most valuable purchase he ever made in his life. The rules were these: *Keep the head cool; Keep the feet warm; Take a light supper; Rise early.*

The old word for "holy" in the German language also means "healthy," and, in our own, "hale," "whole," and "holy" are from the same root. Carlyle says that "you could not get any better definition of what 'holy' really is than 'healthy—completely healthy.'" *Mens sana in corpore sano.* There is no kind of achievement you could make in the world that is equal to perfect health. What are nuggets and millions? The French financier said, "Alas! why is there no sleep to be sold?" Sleep was not in the market at any quotation.

What boots it to have attained wealth, if the wealth is accompanied by ceaseless ailments? What is the worth of distinction, if it has brought hypochondria with it? Surely no one needs telling that a good digestion, a bounding pulse, and high spirits, are elements of happiness which no external advantages can out-balance. Chronic bodily disorder casts a gloom over the brightest prospects; while the vivacity of strong health gilds even misfortune. Health is not merely freedom from bodily pain; it is the capability of receiving pleasure from all surrounding things, and from the employment of all our faculties. It need scarcely be said that without this capability even marriage cannot make us happy. Indeed, without a fair share of health to start with people are not justified in taking upon themselves the responsibilities of matrimony, and running the risk of introducing into the world weak children that may be said to be damned rather than born into it.

It has been remarked that the first requisite to success in life is to be a good animal. Will it seem shockingly unpoetical to suggest that this is also a very important element of success in marriage? Certainly beauty has great power in retaining as well as in gaining affection, and health is a condition of beauty. A clear complexion and laughing eyes, a supple and rounded form, and a face unmarked by wrinkles of pain or peevishness, are the results of vigour of constitution.

Overflowing health produces good humour, and we all know how important that is to matrimonial felicity. I once knew an old lady who used to say that it was a duty to sometimes take medicine for the sake of one's friends. She was thinking of the effect of dyspepsia, congested liver, and other forms of ill-health upon our tempers. The chief misery of dyspepsia is that it is not merely pain, but pain which affects the intellect and feelings alike; in Carlyle's vivid words: "Every window of your feeling, even of your intellect, as it were, begrimed and mud-bespattered, so that no pure ray can enter; a whole drug-shop in your inwards; the foredone soul drowning slowly in the quagmires of disgust."

Oliver Wendell Holmes speaks of a man in the clothing business with an impressible temperament who let a customer "slip through his fingers one day without fitting him with a new garment. 'Ah!' said he to a friend of mine, who was standing by, 'if it hadn't been for that confounded headache of mine this morning, I'd have had a coat on that man, in spite of himself, before he left the store.' A passing throb only; but it deranged the nice mechanism required to persuade the accidental human being, *x*, into a given piece of broadcloth, *a*."

How many more happy days would a husband and wife spend together were it not for confounded headaches which cause foolish, bitter words to be spoken. If a man cannot do business when the nice mechanism of his body is deranged, neither can he be gentle and kind in the family circle. This is what Dr. Johnson meant when he said that a man is a villain when sick.

"Smelfungus," says Sterne, "had been the grand tour, and had seen nothing to admire; all was barren from Dan to Beersheba; and when I met him he fell foul of the Venus de Medici; and abused her ladyship like a common fish-fag. 'I will tell it,' cried he, 'I will tell it to the world!' 'You had better,' said Sterne, 'tell it to your physician.'" So too when a man falls foul of his wife, and abuses her ladyship like a common fish-fag because his liver is out of order, he had better go to a physician and take every means of clearing his clouded temper.

How much a husband can do by sympathy and kindness for a sick wife! Mrs. Carlyle used to say, "The very least attention from Carlyle just glorifies me. When I have one of my headaches, and the sensation of red-hot knitting-needles darting into my brain, Carlyle's way of expressing sympathy is to rest a heavy hand on the top of my head, and keep it there in perfect silence for several seconds, so that although I could scream with nervous agony, I sit like a martyr, smiling with joy at such a proof of profound pity from him." The truth is that happiness is the most powerful of tonics. By accelerating the circulation of the blood, it facilitates the performance of every function; and so tends alike to increase health when it exists, and to restore it when it has been lost.

If acts of kindness from a husband are necessary in all cases, they are especially so in cases of his wife's illness, from whatever cause arising, and most of all when there is a prospect of her becoming a mother. This is the time for him to show care, watchful tenderness, attention to all her wishes, and anxious efforts to quiet her fears. Any agitation or fatigue at such times may cause the remaining years of her life to be years of pain and weakness. If he value happiness in married life and would escape bitter self-reproach, the husband will be very careful of his wife when in this condition. And it is the duty of the young wife, on her part, to take care of her own health, because of the manner in which hers will affect the health of her expected child. And as the moral and mental nature of the child is scarcely less dependent on her than the physical, she should cherish only such mental frames and dispositions as she would like to see reproduced in her child. How much her husband can help or hinder her in doing so! Then when the child is born she ought if possible to give it the food which nature provides and which is its birthright. No other is so congenial, and the consequences of unnatural methods of feeding are sometimes most injurious to the bodies and minds of children.

In these hard times of great competition in every kind of business, it is a sad fact that many men have to overwork themselves, or at least fancy they have, in order to get a living for their families. But there are others who kill themselves by overwork and over-anxiety, for what? To amass more money than they can well spend, or to catch the soap-bubble called fame—

"And all to leave what with his tact he won,
To that unfeathered two-legged thing, a son."

Alas! that such men never think of His considerate words to His disciples who was the great Physician of the body as well as of the soul—"Come ye apart, and rest awhile." If they did they would be able to show to their friends at home what the Lord had done for them. Rest to their overstrung nerves would make them less peevish, discontented, and generally disagreeable.

More open-air amusements, and more indoor gaiety, would save a great many failing brains and enfeebled hearts.

Of course health may be impaired quite as much by doing too little work as by doing too much. This truth was enforced by Thackeray, when, addressing a medical friend, he exclaimed, "Doctor, there is not in the whole of your pharmacopœia so sovereign a remedy as hard work." All depends upon the temperament and constitution. What kills one man cures another. General Sir Charles Napier, who was not physically a strong man, declared that for the first time he had discovered what total immunity from "malaise" meant when he took to working seventeen hours a day at Cephalonia, as acting Governor or Commissioner of the Ionian Islands.

Not all but by far the largest part of the cure of nervous depression rests with the patient. Change, exercise, fresh air, diet, tonics—all these together will not cure any one who gives up and gives way.

Above all, we should try to be cheerful. A clerical friend, at a celebrated watering-place, met a lady who seemed hovering on the brink of the grave. Her cheeks were hollow and wan, her manner listless, her step languid, and her brow wore the severe contraction so indicative both of mental and physical suffering, so that she was to all observers an object of sincere pity. Some years afterward he encountered this same lady; but so bright, and fresh, and youthful, so full of healthful buoyancy, and so joyous in expression, that he questioned the lady if he had not deceived himself with regard to identity. "Is it possible," said he, "that I see before me Mrs. B. who presented such a doleful appearance at the Springs several years ago?" "The very same." "And pray tell me the secret of your cure. What means did you use to attain to such vigour of mind and body, to such cheerfulness and rejuvenation?" "A very simple remedy," returned she, with a beaming face; "I stopped worrying and began to laugh; that was all."

We would call the attention of heads of families to the following mistakes which the "Sanitary Record" lately enumerated: "It is a mistake to labour when you are not in a fit condition to do so. To think that the more a person eats the healthier and stronger he will become. To go to bed at midnight and rise at daybreak, and imagine that every hour taken from sleep is an hour gained. To imagine that if a little work or exercise is good, violent or prolonged exercise is better. To conclude that the smallest room in the house is large enough to sleep in. To eat as if you only had a minute to finish the meal in, or to eat without an appetite, or continue after it has been satisfied, merely to satisfy the taste. To believe that children can do as much work as grown people, and that the more hours they study the more they learn. To imagine that whatever remedy causes one to feel immediately better (as alcoholic stimulants) is good for the system, without regard to the after-effects. To take off proper clothing out of season because you have become heated. To sleep exposed to a direct draught in any season. To think that any nostrum or patent medicine is a specific for all the diseases flesh is heir to."

There are few things more important to health than the due adjustment of play and work. The school at which a boy ten years of age is made to work at his tasks for the same time as a lad of sixteen ought to be avoided by all parents. If health is to be preserved in early youth, the child must be treated on the same principle as a foal would be. He, or she, must be allowed to a great extent to "run wild," and "lessons" must be carefully graduated to the bodily powers.

Those mothers who are inclined to dose their children too much should be reminded that it was during the days when physic flourished in the nursery that the greatest amount of disease was found. It is not by medicine, but by acting in accordance with natural laws, that health of body and health of mind and morals can be secured at home. Without a knowledge of such laws, the mother's love too often finds its recompense only in the child's coffin.

In the management of their children's health some mothers are guided by everybody and everything except by nature herself. And yet the child's healthy instincts are what alone should be followed.

Sir Samuel Garth, physician to George I., was a member of the Kit-Kat Club. Coming to the club one night, he said he must soon be gone, having many patients to attend; but some good wine being produced, he forgot them. Sir Richard Steele was of the party, and reminded him of the visits he had to pay. Garth pulled out his list, which amounted to fifteen, and said, "It's no great matter whether I see them to-night or not; for nine of them have such bad constitutions that all the physicians in the world can't save them; and the other six have such good constitutions that all the physicians in the world can't kill them."

Probably the carelessness of many people about their health may be explained in the same way. They think either that their constitutions are so good that nothing can injure them or else that they are so bad that nothing can make them better. And often it is a bottle of wine or some other indulgence of appetite that keeps health away. We have heard of a well-known character who, having had many severe attacks of gout, and who, getting into years, and having a cellar of old port wine, upon which he drew somewhat considerably, was advised by his physician to give up the port, and for the future to drink a certain thin claret not very expensive. Said the gentleman in reply to this suggestion: "I prefer my gout with my port, to being cured of my gout with that claret of yours!" Of a delicate man who would not control his appetite it was said, "One of his passions which he will not resist is for a particular dish, pungent, savoury, and multifarious, which sends him almost every night into Tartarus." Talking of the bad effects of late hours Sydney Smith said of a distinguished diner-out that it would be written on his tomb, "He dined late." "And died early," added Luttrell.

Such people ought to be told that in playing tricks with their health they are committing a very great sin. "Perhaps," says Mr. Herbert Spencer, "nothing will so much hasten the time when body and mind will both be adequately cared for, as a diffusion of the belief that the preservation of health is a *duty*. Few seem conscious that there is such a thing as physical morality. Men's habitual words and acts imply the idea that they are at liberty to treat their bodies as they please. Disorders entailed by disobedience to Nature's dictates, they regard simply as grievances, not as the effects of a conduct more or less flagitious. Though the evil consequences inflicted on their dependents, and on future generations, are often as great as those caused by crime; yet they do not think themselves in any degree criminal. It is true that, in the case of drunkenness, the viciousness of a bodily transgression is recognized; but none appear to infer that, if this bodily transgression is vicious, so too is every bodily transgression. The fact is, that all breaches of the laws of health are *physical sins.*"

Certainly there are many great sufferers who are not responsible for their ailments, and sometimes they teach lessons of patience and resignation so well in the world and in their families, that their work is quite as valuable as that of the active and healthy. Robert Hall, being troubled with an acute disease which sometimes caused him to roll on the floor with agony, would rise therefrom, wiping from his brow the drops of sweat which the pain had caused, and, trembling from the conflict, ask, "But I did not complain—I did not cry out much, did I?"

Sydney Smith may have dined out more than was good for his health, but he never allowed infirmities to sour his temper. At the end of a letter to an old friend he adds playfully, "I have gout, asthma, and seven other maladies, but am otherwise very well." For the sake of domestic happiness let us preserve our health; but when we do get ill we should endeavour to bear it in this cheerful spirit.

CHAPTER XXVII.

LOVE SURVIVING MARRIAGE.

"Thou leanest thy true heart on mine,
And bravely bearest up!
Aye mingling Love's most precious wine
In life's most bitter cup!
And evermore the circling hours
New gifts of glory bring;
We live and love like happy flowers,
All in our fairy ring.

We have known a many sorrows, sweet!
We have wept a many tears,
And after trod with trembling feet
Our pilgrimage of years.
But when our sky grew dark and wild,
All closelier did we cling;
Clouds broke to beauty as you smiled,
Peace crowned our fairy ring."—*Massey.*

Marriage is sometimes said to be the door that leads deluded mortals back to earth; but this need not and ought not to be the case. Writing to his wife from the sea-side, where he had gone in search of health, Kingsley said: "This place is perfect; but it seems a dream and imperfect without you. Blessed be God for the rest, though I never before felt the loneliness of being without the beloved being whose every look and word and motion are the key-notes of my life. People talk of love ending at the altar.... Fools!"

Of course the enthusiastic tempestuous love of courting days will not as a rule remain. A married couple soon get to feel towards each other very much as two chums at college, or two partners in a business who are at the same time old and well-tried friends. Young married people often think that those who have been in the holy state of matrimony twenty or thirty years longer than themselves are very prosy, unromantic, and by no means perfect examples of what married people ought to be. We would remind persons manifesting this newly-married intolerance of what an old minister of the Church of Scotland once said to a young Scotch Dissenter who was finding many faults—"When your lum (chimney) has reeked as long as ours perhaps it will have as much soot."

"There is real love just as there are real ghosts; every person speaks of it; few persons have seen it." This cynical remark of Rochefoucauld is certainly not true in reference to love before marriage and the existence of love even after it rests on far better evidence than the existence of ghosts. I have never seen a ghost, but I have seen love surviving matrimony, and I have read amongst very many other instances the following.

Old Robert Burton relates several cases of more than lovers' love existing between husband and wife. He tells us of women who have died to save their husbands, and of a man who, when his wife was carried away by Mauritanian pirates, became a galley-slave in order to be near her. Of a certain Rubenius Celer he says that he "would needs have it engraven on his tomb that he had led his life with Ennea, his dear wife, forty-three years and eight months, and never fell out." After twenty-eight years' experience, Faraday spoke of his marriage as "an event which more than any other had contributed to his earthly happiness and healthy state of mind." For forty-six years the union continued unbroken; the love of the old man remaining as fresh, as earnest, and as heart-whole, as in the days of his youth. Another man of science, James Nasmyth, the inventor of the steam-hammer, had a similar happy experience. "Forty-two years of married life finds us the same devoted 'cronies' that we were at the beginning." Dr. Arnold often dwelt upon "the rare, the unbroken, the almost awful happiness" of his domestic life, and carried the first feelings of enthusiastic love and watchful care through twenty-two years of wedded life.

There are such things as love-letters between married people. Here are two extracts from one written by Caroline Perthes to her absent husband: "I have just looked out into the night, and thought of thee. It is a glorious night, and the stars are glittering above me, and if in thy carriage one appears to thee brighter than the rest, think that it showers down upon thee love and kindness from me, and no sadness, for I am not now unhappy when you are absent. Yet I am certain that this does not proceed from any diminution of affection. If I could only show how I feel towards you, it would give you joy. After all I may say or write, it is still unexpressed, and far short of the living love which I carry in my heart. If you could apprehend me without words, you would understand me better. The children do their best, but you are always the same, and have ever the first place in my heart. Thank God, my Perthes, neither time nor circumstances can ever affect my love to you; my affection knows neither youth nor age, and is eternal."

If love never survived matrimony would Mrs. Carlyle have written a letter like the following which she did to a friend who made a special effort to console her soon after the death of her mother?—"Only think of my husband, too, having given me a little present! he who never attends to such nonsenses as birthdays, and who dislikes nothing in the world so much as going into a shop to buy anything, even his own trousers and coats; so that, to the consternation of cockney tailors, I am obliged to go about them. Well, he actually risked himself in a jeweller's shop, and bought me a very nice smelling-bottle! I cannot tell you how *wae* his little gift made me, as well as glad; it was the first thing of the kind he ever gave me in his life. In great matters he is always kind and considerate? but these little attentions, which we women attach so much importance to, he was never in the habit of rendering to any one; his up-bringing, and the severe turn of mind he has from nature, had alike indisposed him towards them. And now the desire to replace to me the irreplaceable makes him as good in little things as he used to be in great."

Carlyle never forgot her birthday afterwards. Once she thought that he had, and she told the story of her mistake and its correction thus: "Oh! my dear husband, fortune has played me such a cruel trick this day! and I do not even feel any resentment against fortune for the suffocating misery of the last two hours. I know always, when I seem to you most exacting, that whatever happens to me is nothing like so bad as I deserve. But you shall hear how it was. Not a line from you on my birthday, the postmistress averred! I did not burst out crying, I did not faint—did not do anything absurd, so far as I know; but I walked back again, without speaking a word; and with such a tumult of wretchedness in my heart as you, who know me, can conceive. And then I shut myself in my own room to fancy everything that was most tormenting. Were you, finally, so out of patience with me that you had resolved to write to me no more at all? Had you gone to Addiscombe, and found no leisure there to remember my existence? Were you taken ill, so ill that you could not write? That last idea made me mad to get off to the railway, and back to London. Oh, mercy! what a two hours I had of it! And just when I was at my wits' end, I heard Julia crying out through the house: 'Mrs. Carlyle, Mrs. Carlyle! Are you there? Here is a letter for you.' And so there was after all! The postmistress had overlooked it, and had given it to Robert, when he went afterwards, not knowing that we had been. I wonder what love-letter was ever received with such thankfulness! Oh, my dear! I am not fit for living in the world with this organization. I am as much broken to pieces by that little accident as if I had come through an attack of cholera or typhus fever. I cannot even steady my hand to write decently. But I felt an irresistible need of thanking you, by return of post. Yes, I have kissed the dear little card-case; and now I will lie down awhile, and try to get some sleep. At least, to quiet myself, I will try to believe—oh, why cannot I believe it once for all—that, with all my faults and follies, I am 'dearer to you than any earthly creature.'"

Hundreds of other cases of love surviving matrimony might be cited but we shall only add one more. On the fifty-fourth anniversary of his marriage, Mr. S. C. Hall composed the following lines, a copy of which I had the pleasure of receiving from himself:

"Yes! we go gently down the hill of life,
And thank our God at every step we go;
The husband-lover and the sweetheart-wife.
Of creeping age what do we care or know?

Each says to each, 'Our fourscore years, thrice told,
Would leave us young:' the soul is never old!

What is the grave to us? can it divide
The destiny of two by God made one?
We step across, and reach the other side,
To know our blended life is but begun.
These fading faculties are sent to say
Heaven is more near to-day than yesterday."

CHAPTER XXVIII.

"HE WILL NOT SEPARATE US, WE HAVE BEEN SO HAPPY."

"To veer how vain! on, onward strain,
Brave barks! in light, in darkness too;
Through winds and tides one compass guides,
To that, and your own selves, be true.

But, O blithe breeze! and O great seas,
Though ne'er that earliest parting past
On your wide plain they join again,
Together lead them home at last.

One port, methought, alike they sought,
One purpose hold where'er they fare.
O bounding breeze, O rushing seas!
At last, at last unite them there!"—*Clough.*

"He will not separate us, we have been so happy"—these were the last words of Charlotte Brontë when, having become Mrs. Nicholls, and having lived with her husband only nine months, death came to snatch the cup of domestic felicity from the lips of the happy pair. A low wandering delirium came on. Wakening for an instant from this stupor, she saw her husband's woe-worn face, and caught the sound of some murmured words of prayer that God would spare her. "Oh!" she whispered, "I am not going to die, am I? He will not separate us, we have been so happy."

Mrs. Elizabeth Fry, when a girl, loved her family so dearly that she used to wish that when they had to die, two large walls might press towards each other, and crush them all, that they might die all together, and be spared the misery of parting. Loving husbands and wives will sympathize with this wish, for they must sometimes look forward with dread to the misery of parting from each other.

"To know, to esteem, to love—and then to part,
Makes up life's tale to many a feeling heart!"

In all ages the anticipation and the reality of separation has been the greatest and sometimes the only sorrow in the lot of united couples. Many very touching inscriptions have been found in the Catacombs at Rome, but none more touching than those which record this separation. Here is one of them. It is in memory of a very young wife, who must have been married when little more than a child (fourteen), and then left by her husband, a soldier, called off probably to serve in the provinces. He returns to find his poor little wife dead. Was she martyred or did she fret herself to death, or was she carried off with malaria in the Catacombs? We know nothing; but here is her epitaph full of simple pathos, and warm as with the very life blood: "To Domina, 375 A.D., my sweetest and most innocent wife, who lived sixteen years and four months, and was married two years, with whom I was not able to live more than six months, during which time I showed her my love as I felt it; none else so loved each other." When Sir Albert Morton died, his wife's grief was such that she shortly followed him, and was laid by his side. Wotton's two lines on the event have been celebrated as containing a volume in seventeen words:

"He first deceased; she for a little tried
To live without him, liked it not, and died."

When Colonel Hutchinson, the noble Commonwealth officer, felt himself dying, knowing the deep sorrow which his death would occasion to his wife, he left this message, which was conveyed to her: "Let her, as she is above other women, show herself on this occasion a good Christian, and above the pitch of ordinary women." Faithful to his injunction, instead of lamenting his loss, she indulged her sorrow in depicting her husband as he had lived. "They who dote on mortal excellences," she says, in her Introduction to the "Life," "when, by the inevitable fate of all things frail, their adored idols are taken from them, may let loose the winds of passion to bring in a flood of sorrow, whose ebbing tides carry away the dear memory of what they have lost; and when comfort is essayed to such mourners, commonly all objects are removed out of their view which may with their remembrance renew the grief; and in time these remedies succeed, and oblivion's curtain is by degrees drawn over the dead face; and things less lovely are liked, while they are not viewed together with that which was most excellent. But I, that am under a command not to grieve at the common rate of desolate women, while I am studying which way to moderate my woe, and if it were possible to augment my love, I can for the present find out none more just to your dear father, nor consolatory to myself, than the preservation of his memory, which I need not gild with such flattering commendations as hired preachers do equally give to the truly and titularly honourable. A naked undressed narrative, speaking the simple truth of him, will deck him with more substantial glory than all the panegyrics the best pens could ever consecrate to the virtues of the best men."

When death removed Stella from Swift, and he was left alone to think of what he had lost, he described her as "the truest, most virtuous, and valuable friend, that I, or perhaps any other person, was ever blessed with." Henceforward he must strive and suffer alone. The tenderness, of which his attachment to Stella had been the strongest symptom, deeply as it had struck its roots into his nature, withered into cynicism. But a lock of Stella's hair is said to have been found in Swift's desk, when his own fight was ended, and on the paper in which it was wrapped were written words that have become proverbial for the burden of pathos that their forced brevity seems to hide—"Only a woman's hair." It is for each reader to read his own meaning into them.

Dr. Johnson's wife was querulous, exacting, old, and the reverse of beautiful, and yet a considerable time after her death he said that ever since the sad event he seemed to himself broken off from mankind; a kind of solitary wanderer in the wild of life, without any direction or fixed point of view; a gloomy gazer on the world to which he had little relation. After recording some good resolution in his Journal he was in the habit since her death of writing after it his wife's name—"Tetty." It is only a word; but how eloquent it is! When a certain Mr. Edwards asked him if he had ever known what it was to have a wife, Johnson replied: "Sir, I have known what it was to have a wife, and (in a solemn, tender, faltering tone) I have known what it was to *lose a wife*. I had almost broke my heart." Nor did he allow himself to forget this experience. To New Year's Day, Good Friday, Easter Day, and his own birthday, which he set apart as sacred days dedicated to solemn thought and high communion with his own soul, he added *the day of his wife's death*.

Nor are such separations less felt in humble life. A year or two ago the newspapers in describing a colliery accident related that upon the tin water-bottle of one of the dead men brought out of the Seaham Pit, there was scratched, evidently with a nail, the following letter to his wife: "DEAR MARGARET,—There was forty of us altogether at 7 A.M., some was singing hymns, but my thought was on my little Michael. I thought that him and I would meet in heaven at the same time. Oh, dear wife, God save you and the children, and pray for myself. Dear wife, farewell. My last thoughts are about you and the children. Be sure and learn the children to pray for me. Oh, what a terrible position we are in.—MICHAEL SMITH, 54, Henry Street." The little Michael he refers to was his child whom he had left at home ill. The lad died on the day of the explosion.

A writer on *The Orkneys and Shetland* tells the following. A native of Hoy went one day to his minister and said, "Oh! sir, but the ways of Providence are wonderful! I thought I had met with a sair misfortune when I lost baith my coo and my wife at aince over the cliff, twa months sin; but I gaed over to Graemsay, and I hae gotten a far better coo and a far bonnier wife."

That a wife is not always so easily replaced is evident from the following letter which appeared in the Belfast papers: "SIR,—I request permission to inform your readers of the fair sex that I have just received a letter from a young man residing in a rapidly-rising town of a few months' growth, and terminus of several railways, in one of the Western States of America, telling me that he has lost his wife, and would wish to get another one—a nice little Irish girl, just like the other one; that she should be 'between twenty and twenty-five years of age, of good habits, of good forme, vertchaus, and a Protestant.' My correspondent, who is a perfect stranger to me, informs me that he is 28 years of age, and 'ways' 150 lbs.; that he is a carpenter by trade, and owns a farm of 65 acres, and that he can give the best of references. I am writing to him for his references and his photograph, and also for a photograph and description of his late wife, on receipt of which I will address you again.—VERE FOSTER, Belfast, Jan. 5, 1883."

This poor, uneducated carpenter was so happy with his nice little Irish girl that when taken from him he could not help trying to get another one just like her, and sends more than three thousand miles for a chip of the old block. If any blame him for seeking for a second wife let them reflect on the awful solitude of a backwoods settlement when the prairie flower represented by a nice little Irish girl had faded and died. By desiring to marry again he paid the highest compliment to his first wife, for he showed that she had made him a happy man.

It is sometimes said that the happiest days of a man's life is the day of his wedding and the day of his wife's funeral. And the *Quarterly Review*, in an article on Church Bells, related that one Thomas Nash in 1813 bequeathed fifty pounds a year to the ringers of the Abbey Church at Westminster, "on condition of their ringing on the whole peal of bells, with clappers muffled, various *solemn and doleful changes* on the 14th of May in every year, being the anniversary of my wedding-day; and also on the anniversary of my decease to ring a grand bob-major, and *merry, mirthful peals*, unmuffled, in joyful commemoration of my happy release from domestic tyranny and wretchedness."

As a rule, however, no matter how much a husband and wife have tormented each other the separation when it comes is very painful. How true to life is Trollope's description of the effect of Mrs. Proudie's death upon the bishop. "A wonderful silence had come upon him which for the time almost crushed him. He would never hear that well-known voice again! He was free now. Even in his misery—for he was very miserable—he could not refrain from telling himself that. No one could now press uncalled for into his study, contradict him in the presence of those before whom he was bound to be authoritative, and rob him of all his dignity. There was no one else of whom he was afraid. She had at least kept him out of the hands of other tyrants. He was now his own master, and there was a feeling—I may not call it of relief, for as yet there was more of pain in it than of satisfaction—a feeling as though he had escaped from an old trouble at a terrible cost, of which he could not as yet calculate the amount.... She had in some ways, and at certain periods of his life, been very good to him. She had kept his money for him and made things go straight when they had been poor. His interests had always been her interests. Without her he would never have been a bishop. So, at least, he told himself now, and so told himself probably with truth. She had been very careful of his children. She had never been idle. She had never been fond of pleasure. She had neglected no acknowledged duty. He did not doubt that she was now on her way to heaven. He took his hands down from his head, and clasping them together, said a little prayer. It may be doubted, whether he quite knew for what he was praying. The idea of praying for her soul, now that she was dead, would have scandalized him. He certainly was not praying for his own soul. I think he was praying that God might save him from being glad that his wife was dead.... But yet his thoughts were very tender to her. Nothing reopens the springs of love so fully as absence, and no absence so thoroughly as that which must needs be endless. We want that which we have not; and especially that which we can never have. She had told him in the very last moments of her presence with him that he was wishing that she were dead, and he had made her no reply. At the moment he had felt, with savage anger, that such was his wish. Her words had now come to pass, and he was a widower; and he assured himself that he would give all that he possessed in the world to bring her back again."

Richard Cobden once asked in reference to a famous and successful but unscrupulous statesman, "How will it be with him when all is retrospect?" Husband and wife, how will it be when death has separated you, and your married life is retrospect?

Many a man or woman, going on from day to day in the faithful performance of duty, without any sweet token of approval to cheer the sometimes weary path, would find it act as the very wine of life could he or she only hear by anticipation some few of the passionate words of appreciation or regret that will be spoken when the faithful heart, stilled for ever, can no longer be moved by the tone of loving commendation. Do not in this way let us keep all the good hermetically sealed up till the supreme touch of death shall force it open.

"Alas! how often at our hearths we see—
And by our side—angels about to be!"

But somehow the selfish absorption of life acts as a soporific to our truer sense, and our "eyes are holden that we do not know them," until, alas! it is too late, and they have "passed out of our sight."

"Could ye come back to me, Douglas, Douglas,
In the old likeness that I knew,
I would be so faithful, so loving, Douglas—
Douglas, Douglas! tender and true!

Never a scornful word should grieve ye,
I'd smile on ye, sweet as the angels do;
Sweet as your smile on me shone ever—
Douglas, Douglas! tender and true."

"The grave buries every error, covers every defect, extinguishes every resentment. From its peaceful bosom spring none but fond regrets and tender recollections. Who can look down upon the grave of an enemy and not feel a compunctious throb that he should have warred with the poor handful of dust that lies mouldering before him?" If the love that is lavished on the graves of dead friends were bestowed on living darlings in equal measure, family life would be a different thing from what it sometimes is.

As George IV. put on the statue of George III. "pater optimus," best of fathers, though he had embittered his father's life, so many a husband tries to relieve his remorse by extravagantly praising the wife who when alive never received any kindness from him. What is hell but truths known too late? and the surviving one of a married pair has to the end of life, if duty in matrimony has been neglected, the incessant wish that something were otherwise than it had been. The one regret to avoid is, that when married life is over, over for ever, to the survivor should come the unutterable but saddening thought, that now, in the late autumn of life, when experience can be no longer of any possible value, he or she understands, at last understands, all that the chivalry of holy matrimony implies and claims on both sides, in manly forbearance, in delicate thoughtfulness, in loving courtesy. Too late now!

Over the triple doorways of the cathedral of Milan there are three inscriptions spanning the splendid arches. Over one is carved a beautiful wreath of roses, and underneath is the legend "All that which pleases is only for a moment." Over the other is a sculptured cross, and there are the words, "All that which troubles is but for a moment." Underneath the great central entrance in the main aisle is the inscription, "That only is which is eternal." Make the most of the happiness of your marriage, and the least of its vexations, for it is a relation that will not last long.

Respice finem, the old monks used to say in their meditations on life. And if we would behave rightly in married life we must "consider the end." Affections are never deepened and refined until the possibility of loss is felt. "Whatsoever thou takest in hand, remember the end, and thou shalt never do amiss." Spare all hard words, omit all slights, for before long there will be a hearse standing at your door that will take away the best friend that you have on earth—a good wife. Then the silence will be appalling; the vacancies ghastly. Reminiscences will rush on the heart like a mountain current over which a cloud has burst. Her jewels, her books, her pictures, her dresses will be put into a trunk and the lid will come down with a heavy thud, as much as to say—"Dead! The morning dead. The night dead. The world dead." Oh! man, if in that hour you think of any unkind word uttered, you will be willing to pay in red coin of blood every drop from your heart, if you could buy it back. Kindly words, sympathizing attentions, watchfulness against wounding the sensitiveness of a wife or husband—it is the omission of these things which is irreparable: irreparable, when we look to the purest enjoyment which might have been our own; irreparable when we consider the compunction which belongs to deeds of love not done.

Carlyle never meant to be unkind to his wife, but in his late years he thought that he had sacrificed her health and happiness in his absorption in his work; that he had been negligent, inconsiderate, and selfish. "For many years after she had left him," writes Mr. Froude, "when he passed the spot where she was last seen alive, he would bare his grey head in the wind and rain—his features wrung with unavailing sorrow. 'Oh!' he often said to me, 'if I could but see her for five minutes to assure her that I had really cared for her throughout all that! But she never knew it, she never knew it!'"

Sorrow, however, may teach us wisdom, and if we study patience in the school of Christ much comfort will from thence be derived. And much hope too. He is the resurrection and the life, and if we believe in Him we believe that there is a Friend in whose arms we ourselves shall fall asleep, and to whose love we may trust for the reunion, sooner or later, of the severed links of sacred human affection.

"And in that perfect Marriage Day
All earth's lost love shall live once more;
All lack and loss shall pass away,
And all find all not found before;
Till all the worlds shall live and glow
In that great love's great overflow."

INDEX.

Printed by Libri Plureos GmbH in Hamburg,
Germany

9 789732 348994